Maa

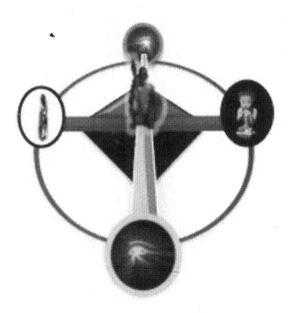

A Guide to the Kamitic Way
for Personal Transformation

By Derric Moore

Four Sons Publications
Liberal, KS
1solalliance.com

Published by: Four Sons Publications
Contact: 1 SoL Alliance Co.
                  P.O. Box 596
                  Liberal, KS 67905-0596
                  www.1solalliance.com

Disclaimer & Legal Notice

The information contained in this book is intended to be educational and not for diagnosis, prescription, or treatment of any health disorder whatsoever. This information should not replace consultation with a competent healthcare professional. The content of the book is intended to be used as an adjunct to a rational and responsible healthcare program prescribed by a licensed healthcare practitioner. This is a book about faith. As such the author and publisher do not warrant the success any person would have using any of the exercises and techniques contained herein. Success and failure will vary. The author and publisher therefore are in no way liable for any misuse of the material contained herein.

To protect the identity and privacy of others, most of the names within this book have been adapted, modified and changed for confidentiality purposes. Any resemblance to real persons, living or dead is purely coincidental.

Cover art and Illustrations by: Derric Moore
Photos Courtesy of Dreamstine.com

ISBN: 978-0-9855067-0-4

Printed in the United States of America

You will free yourself when you learn to be neutral and follow the instructions of your heart without letting things perturb you.

Kamitic Proverb

Also by Derric "Rau Khu" Moore

MAA AANKH: Finding God the Afro-American Spiritual Way, by Honoring the Ancestors and Guardian Spirits

Kamta: The Kamitic Path for Obtaining Power

For additional items and upcoming titles please visit:

www.1solalliance.com

About This Book

Usually when attempting to explain another's cultural philosophy, the tendency is to highlight the similarities between the familiar perspective and the other. In our case, the familiar is usually the Western viewpoint and the unfamiliar is the ancient Egyptian (Kamitic) perspective. Generally speaking anything that is not Western is viewed as being backwards, primitive, and in need of being "saved", which in the past has inspired most literature on the subject to focus upon understanding this cultural perspective from Western viewpoint. Unfortunately, by forcing this philosophy to fit into the Western paradigm it produces a strange set of beliefs that is totally contrary from its origin. Like the strange myth, that Kamit was a society of West Asian invaders that dwelled in Africa and enslaved the indigenous inhabitants to build their civilization. Clearly we can see how ridiculous this sounds, but it has not stopped many scholars from scheming of new theories.

This is why finally, here's a book written about the sacred wisdom of the Kamitic people that doesn't just focus upon theories of what was done thousands of years ago, but upon how to apply those concepts and principles to your life today. In this book, you will learn practical spiritual solutions that you can apply right now to improve your life based upon the author's experience, because the basis of Kamitic spirituality focuses on the power of the mind. Although the Kamitic society is extinct, you can't exist for over 3, 0000 years without making a lasting impression upon the people in that continent. In other words, even though Africa is not homogenous there are certain beliefs and practices from Kamit that have remained unchanged to this very day. Many of these beliefs and practices continue to be applied throughout the Afro – Diaspora. Furthermore, anyone anywhere can implement this unique philosophy into their life, provided they learn how to correctly apply the concepts and principles to their life and live by them.

Unlike Westerners that base their lives upon their limited physical experiences, speculations and theories (proven or unproven), non-Westerners based their lives upon the unlimited ability of the Spirit. This is the foundation of our Truth. In Chinese esoteric it is called the Tao but in the Kamitic language it is called *Maa* (also called Maat), which means balance, law, order, righteousness, truth and the Kamitic "Way of Life". There are many ways to the Maa and the way presented here doesn't promise to be the only guide. It will however present you with the concepts and principles that will help you to awaken your divine potential so that you can obtain real solutions, and discover your own way.

Table of Contents

Acknowledgements

Thank you Almighty God, Nebertcher forall my blessings.

Thanks to my ancestors for the numerous sacrifices that were made and for the priviliges that I am able to enjoy today. Thank you for helping me to better understand the Divine and accept the things I can change and that which is not the will of God.

Thank you netcharu for guarding me and opening the way to my ancestral heritage and legacy.

Thanks to my family and Dulce for your unconditional love, concern, encouragement and support.

And, finally thank you, thank you, thank you Papa, Iya and Ms. B., who wisdom still guides me to this day.

Table of Figures

Preface

Kamitic Spirituality: Developing Faith in the Unknown

It has been said that we are spiritual beings within a physical vessel. Just about every religious order believes this to some extent, but when most of us as children began displaying "extra" ordinary feats that connect us to the spiritual realm, such as seeing angels, and spirits or having premonitions of future events. Most of us as children are criticized, chastised and discouraged by our loved ones from using these normal abilities, because it is deemed as being unacceptable behavior by society. So most of us learn to suppress these spiritual abilities, as some of us learn to view these abilities as talents. While the remaining few because of lack of proper training grow up delusional or mentally unstable.

As a result, we grow up idolizing those individuals (either in fiction or non-fiction) that can perform spiritual feats as a savior, believing that they are superior to us. When in truth, the only reason why these individual can perform these extra ordinary feats is because they have learned how to train their mind.

It doesn't dawn us what has been done until we begin to see that our universe is composed of a physical and spiritual (non-physical) reality, which means in short that physical things can't bring us peace, happiness, love, etc. In order to acquire these non-physical things we need to go about obtaining them through spiritual means. But, by the time we have realized this we have already suppressed our natural abilities to the point that we forgot that we once had them as children. So, we join some religious order, religious group or denomination. To help us connect back to the Divine what we were before our indoctrination, but the cycle repeats itself because, no one ever tells us. That all of these "extra" ordinary feats such as the ability to interact with non-physical entities, foretell the future, etc. is due to the power of the mind. So with each new generation, the greater society continues to decline because they have not learned how to develop their mind.

I don't have to tell you how bad it is. Anyone can turn on the television, read the newsfeeds and see that slowly but surely people are becoming more and more immoral and unethical. To blame all of the evils in the world on some mythological red impish creature is simply put a cop-out and failure to realize. That people are becoming more immoral because they have no self-discipline, and the reason the number of people lacking self-discipline keeps increasing is because Western society doesn't understand spiritual matters. Here lies the difference between Western and non-Western cultures.

Western culture (in general) simply believes that something does not exist unless it can be "measured" by sight, sound, taste, smell and touch, or proven scientifically. Whereas non-Western cultures (African, Asian, Native American, Latino, etc.) believe in science but also believe that non-physical things exist. The problem with Western belief is that spiritual attributes cannot be measured. If so we would have a mathematical equation for love, faith, hope, charity, etc.? It is the failure to recognize the shortcomings in Western thinking that makes Western behavioral system inadequate in treating spiritual ailments. You cannot cure spiritual ailments by just talking about your problems, praying, reading self-help books or undergoing hypnosis. In order to heal the needs of the soul, you need mental therapy and although there are numerous systems that exist. The Kamitic (Ancient Africans of Egypt) spiritual system I believe was the greatest because it made it possible for the Kamitic society to exist for over three thousand years.

The purpose of this book is to provide the individual practitioner some basic guidelines using Kamitic spirituality for connecting to the Divine. Contrary to popular belief, the Kamitic people did not simply cease to exist when Ancient Egypt fell thousands of years ago by foreign invaders. Many of her inhabitants migrated further into Sub-Sahara Africa where they contributed to the cultural way of life of the people in these regions. While Africa is not homogenous, there are some Kamitic influences that have remained the same for thousands of years. Although, the horrific Transatlantic Slave Trade which carted millions of men, women and children to the Americas, destroyed or severely altered the spiritual systems that were in placed prior to the advent of slavery. These same Kamitic cultural influences continue to exist today throughout the Afro-Diaspora.

The guidelines written within these pages are based upon my personal understanding of the Kamitic culture per my spiritual godfather or *padrino's* teaching of Afro – Cuban culture. Prior to meeting my *padrino*, my understanding of the Kamitic culture was that although the Kamitic people were black and brown Africans. Their culture seemed to be more Middle Eastern, which was certainly not the case. Thanks to my *padrino*

4

(godfather) who was an initiated high priest in the Santeria religion. I got a better understanding of the Kamitic culture and learned that the same core concepts that the Kamitic people used to build their society. Are the same concepts and principles that people who are culturally connected to Africa are still using today. This means that there is no need to imitate, mimic or try to resurrect the past because the core concept and principles are being used today. Although a lot of European and other foreign influences may have been adopted in order for these traditions to survive the onslaught of slavery and racism, the core of all African spiritualties has remained the same and centers on humanity's most important institution – the human family with the backbone of the family being the ancestors.

The ancestors are the backbone of most indigenous practices because we remember our deceased grandparents, aunts, uncles, etc. They (along with our parents) are the ones who instill within us our cultural values. It is therefore harder to upset those whom we love because they help us to understand God. From an Afro – Diaspora perspective, we take literally the commandment, "Honor thy Father and thy Mother" to include all of our elders that have come before us (living and dead). To dishonor our ancestors is to do anything that brings about shame.

Archeologists and some religious orders will tell you that the Kamitic people worshipped numerous deities, had all sorts of secret societies that focused on strange ceremonies, had odd rituals and magical practices, only because these individuals are looking from the outside in and are trying to interpret what our culture was about. Most of these people have a romanticized view of Kamit and its culture equating it with the mystical Atlantis or some other extraordinary reality. When it is understood that the Kamitic people were African people with the similar beliefs and practices as other African people, you'll see that these so-called deities the archeologists speak of are really archetypal ancestors. The various societies are the same secret societies most indigenous cultures have, which are only a mystery or secret to foreigners. The ceremonial rituals are the same type of metaphorical rituals that cultures all over the world practice to instill within its people knowledge of self, and the odd rituals were designed to be that way to help people to learn how to concentrate. In other words, the entire system was to help people to be well balanced and not polarized in one type (right or left brained) thinking.

It should be noted that while the Kamitic people were clearly a highly eccentric culture, they also made numerous scientific discoveries, which contradicts the popular belief that they were a primitive people that believed in a lot of superstitious nonsense. In fact, most successful practitioners in the spiritual arts in contemporary times are usually college educated. The reason is because higher education forces one to develop a strong will in order to succeed in one's courses, which is the same determination one needs to succeed in life. From the Kamitic perspective, which we will see in the future, a weak-minded individual was an evil person because they had no self-control and no self-discipline, so everyone focused on developing him or herself spiritually. They didn't do this by going to school and learning how to be spiritual by taking classes. They did it day by day as a way of life, which is the basis of Kamitic spirituality and the focus of this book.

In case you are wondering why would anyone want to work with his or her ancestors and archetypal ancestors, especially in these times? The answer is because why there may be great solace that comes from giving one's cares and concerns to God. It does not excuse you from accomplishing your destiny. You still have to learn how to love, be charitable, be respectful, ethical, moral and upstanding. You still have to learn responsibility, self-control and self-discipline and this is where the ancestors come in. They help us to learn all of these cultural traits, which help us to become better members of society, and connect to the Divine.

Therefore provided in this book are the essential guidelines to help you to connect with the Divine. Within these pages you will discover how to divine, honor your ancestors and archetypal ancestors. You will learn how to construct an altar for each, as well as work with both to help you with ordinary problems in life. Although all of these practices will help you to develop your mind, the main objective behind this work is to help you to connect to the Divine within your being.

Kamitic Spirituality FAQ's

Since Kamitic spirituality (like most African derived traditions) is an oral and very syncretistic tradition. As there were no texts written explaining how to practice this unique spirituality. The best way to learn this tradition has been through religious syncretism. As a result, it is common to see comparisons drawn between the Kamitic mysteries and the

6

pantheons of similar cultures. Although, there are no specific rules, there are some guidelines that must be followed:

- There is only One Almighty God in the Kamitic spirituality and the Divine's name is Nebertcher, which means "The Lord of All Things," who is the Creator of All Things. The generic name for Nebertcher is Netcher.

- Amun (Amen) Ra, Ra, Khepera, Ra Atum, etc. are not gods nor are they names for the God they are simply attributes of Nebertcher.

- The Power of God or Spirit of Nebertcher is called Rau – the Divine Life Force, which is similar in many ways to the Chinese Chi and the Yoruba Ashe.
- The Kamitic people never worshipped the sun, Atun (Aten); they emulated or made it a major part of their paradigm.

- The ancestors and archetypal ancestors were not worshipped but were highly revered and honored like Catholic saints.

- In Kamitic spirituality, God does not fight the devil because there is no equal to Nebertcher.

- The devil in Kamitic spirituality is not some impish creature running around terrorizing humanity. The devil is called Set and it is a real chaotic energy that fights for control over man and woman's soul.

- In order to practice Kamitic spirituality you have to live your life according to the concepts and principles of Maa.

- In Kamitic spirituality the soul is seen as the immortal part of the human being and when an individual dies, it is the soul that survives death.

- The soul after death does not go to an eternal heaven or hell, because there is no ethereal heaven or a burning pit of fire called

7

hell in Kamitic belief. There is however a higher and lower spiritual realm that exists.

- The higher spiritual realm is where all of our ancestors and spirit guides reside because they learned self-control and self-discipline in life enabling them to be ethical, moral and model citizens for the community. The lower spiritual realm is where all confused, misguided and lost souls reside due to lack of self-control.

- Good behavior does not guarantee that you will ascend to the higher spiritual realms and become an ancestor. In order to ascend to the higher spiritual realms or become an ancestor, one must exercise self – control, self – discipline and self – mastery in life. In other words, to become an ancestor in death one has to live like an ancestor in life. This is where the idea of striving to be Christ-like stems from.

- If an individual has no peace of mind (shame, guilt, heavy heart, etc.) in life because they lived a perverted life ruled by the deviations of Maa (drug abuse, food abuse, sexual perversion, substance abuse, etc.). They will not have peace of mind in death, because one's death is a reflection of the life they lived. The same way you are treated in life is the same way you will be treated in death. If you are ostracized in life because you are involved in immoral, unethical, dangerous and destructive activities and behavior. Your ancestors will ostracize you in death for the same reason, because in essence you are ruled by Set, the Kamitic devil.

- The objective is to strive to become an ancestor in life, so you can reside with the community of ancestors. The way to do this is by working with your ancestors and archetypal ancestors namely Osar.

- We are therefore, spiritual beings incarnated into physical bodies in order to learn spiritual lessons to strengthen the community of ancestors. We are like hunters going into the wild (physical realm) in search of food.

Chapter 1:
Discovering the Ancient Egyptian Way

I'll never forget when I first learned about the power of God within me. I remember it all began when I was a child and was told that I was going to be a preacher like my father when I grew up. In fact my mother named me Derric because she said she knew that I was going to be a leader of some sort, but helping people to find God was the farthest thing from my mind. The reason is because I remembered seeing preachers like my father helplessly trying to save souls with no money or anything in their pockets. Not to mention the fact that "God's shepherds" were always out helping others by sacrificing their time and energy, while rarely spending time with their own family. So, it just infuriated me when people told me that I was supposed to be a preacher and in response. I tried as much as possible to keep from going to church by hiding out in the attic, basement or some other dark place where I could draw surreal images of animals and people from my dreams.

Now, I didn't have anything against the church per se. In fact, as a child I loved listening to the old call and response hymns and the choir singing. What I didn't care for was the classism that existed inside the church, and I especially didn't like the explanation that everything outside of the church was considered a sin and thereby evil. It was a sin to ask questions. It was a sin to listen to secular music. It was a sin to drink. It was a sin to dance. It was a sin to question God. Some of the things like it being a sin to use drugs I easily understood because after seeing the devastation drugs caused (in my community) it made sense, but the other sins I didn't understand why they were considered sins. And, I had serious questions that needed answering. Some of these questions were about the bible like if Adam and Eve were the first people God created and they had two boys Cain and Abel. Who and where did the other people come from that populated the earth? Other questions seemed to be more culturally related, like if good people go to heaven and bad people go to hell. Then where do newborns come from and why when a child displays interesting characteristics did my elders say the child was an old soul?

All of these unanswered questions that I had made me really start to dislike the church. And, when crack cocaine overcame Detroit and tried to destroy every young male in its path. To escape the onslaught I tried to pray for salvation but I felt like my prayers weren't answered because I still got swept up in some of the violence. It wasn't as bad as others had experienced, but it was enough to make me dislike the church. Especially, the early stand that the church took, which was just to pray and hope that everything would be all right.

All of these elements (a lack of understanding about God, questionable faith, the purpose of life, urban socioeconomic issues, etc.) made me wonder if I was just here for God's amusement. Since, it was a sin to question anything because you would be branded a heretic. I had made up in my young mind that since I was going to go to hell in the first place, what was the purpose of living. And, that's when I had my first brief encounter with my guardian angels. Who inspired me to study the ancient Egyptians, so that I could find what worked for them and use it to find God.

So I had to embark upon a long and arduous journey to try and understand the ancient Egyptian religion. Because the ancient Egyptians, whom called themselves Khemau, Kimau, Kemau or Kamau and their country Khamit or Kamit, which from here on out I will refer to, was extinct, had no living priesthood, and no texts explaining what the Kamitic faith was about. So, I read and studied every book that I could find on the subject. Since most of the Kamitic texts at that time were written by archeologists and historians that assumed that the Kamitic people were non-African people and had no clue about African traditions. I had to include in my growing library about Kamit, books on history, metaphysics, mysticism, psychology, religion and self – development. It was through these early years of my research I came across the theory that because early African Americans were so distant from Africa and relocated in a predominantly Protestant Anglo – Saxon society. African Americans lost most of their cultural ties with Africa, which seemed to explain to me why I was treated the way I was in the church.

Subsequently, I also studied Eastern and Western philosophy, and every faith in between. I became a vegan (believing it was the spiritual thing to do), exercised, practiced yoga, treated people nicely, and even worked hard, but it seemed like no matter what I did something was missing. Assuming that I was the problem, I found other people that were interested in the wisdom of Kamit and joined their study groups to help ease my scholastic burden. Then in a sudden turn of events, I got into a bad relationship with an individual who claimed to be a priestess, but after becoming unemployed and homeless due to following her ill advice. After years of being with this individual, it was obvious that she knew nothing about true spirituality. I was angry with her but I was more upset with myself for allowing someone to take advantage of me during my "spiritual naiveté" because they claimed to be "spiritual." I did care about this individual and her children, but it was clear that we were not "soul mates" as she had claimed that the oracle told us we were. I didn't know what to do but I knew that it was time for a change because there was no growth. All I had to show for the eight years I had devoted to reading and studying about the Kamitic religion was an enormous book collection and the ability to cite references. I didn't have a practical understanding of the Kamitic religion as I had originally tried to find. Then out of nowhere, I met an old black man from Cuba, whom I called Papa and that's when everything changed.

Papa and La Manera (The Way)

Papa was a high priest in the Afro – Cuban religion Santeria and a member of the all-male exclusive society Abakua. Even though Papa could not divulge any of his secrets to me, he told me a number of stories about his life that helped him to find his way – la manera or what works for him. Papa was like your typical sage, an older man that spoke in riddles, and told a lot of stories about his lifetime experiences. He shared with me how he felt to fight in the Angolan War and he expressed his mixed views that he had about Castro. One of the most memorable stories that he told was about how when he first came to the United States. While in an encampment with other Cuban refugees, some men wearing white robes and carrying torches rode in on horseback. Papa said that they (Cubans) had never seen anything like it, so they thought it was a parade and that the men were welcoming them into the country; until the men on horseback began attacking them. In the end, they drove the men out, but he said it was that experience that made him realize that even though blacks were discriminated in Cuba. They were not terrorized like they were in America. He continued by saying that he was glad to see other advancements had been made but it was this experience that gave him a different perspective about African Americans.

One of the things I liked about Papa was that he was always explaining himself using Yoruba (West African) and Santeria stories called Pataki, which he had learned in Cuba. At the time, most of the stories he told me about his orishas (the West African equivalent to guardian angels

11

incorrectly called gods and goddesses) seemed to be quite fanciful and entertaining. Even though I could not understand or explain from a rational perspective who or what the orishas were. I enjoyed listening to Papa talk about what he told me was his *la manera*. Papa told me that it is because people don't work with their orishas they don't know their own way. When you don't know your way – what works for you, you tend to follow and do what everyone else does. So, I wrote down what he told me in my journal – *el libro* because he said one day I would need it to find my own *la manera*.

I found the orisha Ellegua to be quite mischievous like a child with good intentions. Chango, the orisha of thunder and fire, whom Papa had told me was my personal orisha, helped me to understand why as a child I got excited during a thunderstorm and would run from tree to tree, when I should have had my backside inside. The orisha of war, hunting and hard work called Oggun, who according to Papa helped Chango fight the devil during a thunderstorm, was sometimes Chango's biggest rival. Oggun reminded me of adventurous younger brother, who built his first by himself at the age of 15, loves to hunt, played semi-professional football, served in the military, is an entrepreneur and truck driver by trade. The orisha of the sea, Yemaya was the only orisha that could truly stop the bitter rival between Chango and Oggun by quelling their fiery tempers with her waters, which reminded me of my mother who would stop the few, fights my brother and I had in our childhood. Obatala, the father of peace, king of the orishas and owner of the sacred white cloth, reminded me of my younger brother, who like Obatala was very slow to anger. In fact, things that would easily upset me, he would let them roll of his back as if it were nothing, but like Obatala, when he finally became angry. All hell would break lose! There were other orishas that Papa told me about like the orisha of tornadoes Oya, who appeared to be my youngest brothers guardian orisha, Ochun the orisha of beauty and sensuality, Babaluaiye the orisha of smallpox and sickness, Ochossi the orisha of the hunt, and many others.

The Real Revolution Begins Within

Shortly after meeting Papa that's when my relationship with "soul mate" ended, but it was on relatively pleasant terms. Deciding it was best that I move, I moved out of the state. When I found a job, I continued to send money to her to help her and the children. I was still upset with her for what she had done, but over time I chalked it up that she didn't know any better, and forgave her. The experience left a bitter taste in my mouth about so-called "spiritual people," because it was a "spiritual person" that took advantage of me. This lesson taught me that regardless of what a person calls themselves, it is their actions that determine who and what they will be.

As a result of the move, I lost contact with Papa, but I would refer back to the stories he taught me every now and then to remind me of the wonderful conversations I use to have with him. I still felt like I didn't know what I was doing but through what Papa had taught me. I didn't really worry about it because I knew in time I would meet someone to help me in my next step. That's when I met an Oshun priestess from the Yoruba tradition that I came to call Iya (Yoruba for Mother). Iya was a gifted seer, unlike tele-psychics that supposedly look into crystal balls or read tarot cards to tell you about your past, present and future. All Iya did was enter into a mild state of trance and she could tell you your whole life story in one to two hours. In one of the consultations she had with me. She told me that the reason my path had been filled with such difficulty, the reason I feel I need to know (experience) everything for myself is because I am refusing to accept my destiny. When I inquired as to what my destiny was she told me that in the Christian sense I was called to be a preacher, which means from a traditional perspective a shaman. I remember that even though everything that Iya had told me about my life was correct, I took her counsel about my destiny lightly and did not heed her warning, which was that if I didn't embrace this path it would get worst.

Then in the summer of 2008 I became deathly ill. Having nothing else to fall back upon, I relied upon these stories that Papa taught me to guide me through the tough times. That's when I was visited by one of my guardian angels, my deceased grandmother. It wasn't like the movies where you see this ghostly flowing figure. It was more like an inner sense or a reassuring hunch that she was near.

Anyway, my grandmother directed my attention to her obituary and when I looked at it. For the first time I noticed that it listed over her birthday "Sunrise" and over her death date "Sunset," which gives the impression that we are all suns just visiting the earth. I had never thought about our life on the planet as being like the sun but it made perfect sense. I wasn't sure how this idea came about but I traced it back to Kongo Angolan people of West Central Africa, who had a cosmogram

13

they called the Dikenga, Tendwa Nza Kongo or Yowa, commonly referred to as the Kongo Cross or Kongo Cosmogram.

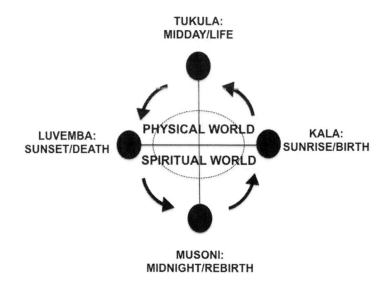

The Kongo Cosmogram

The Kongo Cosmogram according to renowned African scholar, Dr. K. Kia Bunseki Fu-Kiau, was the foundation of the Kongo society. Each end of the cosmogram symbolizing a different moment of the sun meant: Kala (Sunrise/Birth), Tukula (Midday/Life), Luvemba (Sunset/Death) and Musoni (Midnight/Rebirth). The top of the cosmogram was inhabited by the living and represented the physical world, while the bottom half was inhabited by the dead and represented the spiritual world. Graphically speaking, God was imagined as being at the top and ancestral dead below.

The cosmogram could be interpreted in a number of ways and was the basis of the Kongo spiritual tradition. Generally speaking it meant that any time a person experiences setbacks such as in the case of a lawsuit or has grave misfortunes in their life. They were experiencing a little death and therefore had to reborn in order to overcome the ordeal. A little death from the Kongo perspective versus the big death – the end of physical life, was interpreted as an initiation, resulting in a change of consciousness. A change in consciousness occurs whenever you see the consequences of your actions or the errors of your way. As a result, you purposely choose not to engage in the destructive action or behavior any more by standing in the middle of the crossroads and swear an oath in between God and your ancestors. Therefore, spiritual growth occurred by simply observing sacred oaths that were made and respecting taboos.

Then I began to remember in the *Story of Ra and Oset* that when Ra was asked to reveal his true name he told Oset that, "I am KhepeRA in the morning, I am RA at noon, and I am Tmu at evening" before finally revealing his name to her. That's when I realized that the so – called Kamitic sun gods were not gods at all but, just like the Kongo Cosmogram, they represented different moments of the sun in the Kamitic language. Following the gentle insinuation from my ancestress (my grandmother), I compared the Kongo Cosmogram to the Kamitic philosophies, myths and legends and found that the four moments of the sun in the Kamitic language are: Khepera (Sunrise/Birth), Ra (Midday/Life), Tmu was also called Atum or Ra Atum (Sunset/Death) and Amun Ra (Midnight/Rebirth).

At that moment two things became clear to me. The first was that my grandmother shared this insight with me to inform me. That because of my illness I was clearly at the Ra Atum (Sunset/Death) stage in the cycle of my life. My sun was setting and I was knocking at Death's Doors. And second, that the question on rather I lived or died depended totally upon the next choice or decision I made. Needless to say, I chose to live, but like all great heroes and heroines who make the decision to be reborn I had to undergo some changes. I knew I could no longer live my life the way I had in the past. There were some things (attitudes, behaviors, beliefs, ideas, thoughts, viewpoints, etc.) in my life I had to get rid of in order to be reborn. I didn't exactly know what they all were but I had to have faith that I would get through this phase.

Now, the interesting thing about this whole phenomenon is that I would not have even discovered this pattern if it weren't for my grandmother, who proved to me that she, was physically dead but her soul did not die. The other interesting thing about this was that I didn't know anything about angels. I grew up somewhat believing that they existed and I had heard other people talk about them in church when I was a kid. But I never had any practical experience with angels. This experience forced me to conclude that the reason I had this experience was because of what Papa had taught me. So, when I went back and reviewed everything that he told me that I wrote in my *libro*. That's when I began to realize that even though Papa did not study history, religion and

15

all of the other books that I had read. He knew a great deal about spirituality and saw that I was in a disturbed state because of my erroneous beliefs, which created my present paradigm.

Some of these beliefs I had were from my own doing, but most of these negative beliefs were indiscriminately learned from my parents, extended family, school, church, the community, society, etc. Meaning I imitated a lot of these beliefs subconsciously when I was child because this is what a child does until his or her conscious mind develops. I had come across this subject before and the first time I heard it I became angry with my parents thinking that they didn't teach me correctly. This new understanding forced me to see. That my parents could only teach me what they saw and thought was best for me. So I apologize to them and forgave myself for the misunderstanding, which healed me of the bitterness I had for Christianity. It also helped me to see the contributions made by my Christian ancestors and brought me closer to my ancestral legacy.

That's when I realized that in his own unique little way, Papa told me all of those stories because he was sowing within me the seeds of spiritual change, to create a shift in my paradigm. As the revolution within me began, my grandmother stayed with me in mind and inspired me to read again, the *Story of Ra and Oset*.

Baptized by Fire

In the story Oset wanted Ra's power to do whatsoever she willed, so she created a serpent to bite the great king and bring sickness into his body. The plan was that in order for Ra to heal himself he would have to reveal his sacred name to her. When Ra made his daily survey across the land he came across the serpent, which bit him and made him gravely ill. He called all of his children to his side and asked that they remove the poison that was moving through his body, but none were able to provide him with a remedy. Then, Oset appeared and asked Ra to reveal his sacred name so that she could drive the poison from his body. In the grip of his agony, Ra told Oset.

"I have made the heavens and the earth, I have ordered the mountains, I have created all that is above them, I have made the water, I have made to come into being the great and wide sea, I have made the 'Bull of his mother,' from whom spring the delights of love. I have made the heavens, I have stretched out the two horizons like a curtain, and I have placed the soul of the

16

gods within them. I am he who, if he openeth his eyes, doth make the light, and, if he closeth them, darkness cometh into being. At his command the Nile riseth, and the gods know not his name. I have made the hours, I have created the days, I bring forward the festivals of the year, I create the Nile-flood. I make the fire of life, and I provide food in the houses. I am KhepeRA in the morning, I am RA at noon, and I am Tmu at evening."

After Ra's tirade, Oset told the great king that the poison remained in his body because he had not relinquished his sacred name. Finally, after much deliberation, Ra decided to tell her his name but he would only do so in secret.

It took me a while to understand this story in its entirety but when the mystic light bulb finally came on. I began to see that the same way Ra revealed his name (a symbol of God's grace and power) to Oset in secret, it was the only way I could receive God's grace and understand the Kamitic mysteries. The secret that was passed to Oset was hidden, which was a pun on the name Amun Ra – the Hidden Ra. In other words, the reason I couldn't comprehend the Kamitic wisdom or make practical understanding of it, was because there was a cultural barrier preventing me from doing so. In order to truly learn about another's culture when you are not born into it is by being initiated.

It instantly became evident to me that because God, the Almighty is most inconceivable, incomprehensible and unimaginable being in existence. God uses archetypes to communicate his will, because if God revealed itself to us. It would literally blow our finite mind, because the Divine is beyond our intellectual comprehension. There are no words in our language that can truly define and explain who or what the Almighty is which is what I had to learn. Once, I began to accept this truth, I understood wholeheartedly why Ra had to share his name to Oset in secret and why even in the Old Testament. Moses is told by the Great I AM to warn the people not to gaze upon them because they would perish.

I was clearly perishing from a metaphorical perspective because I had not been initiated. But, how was I going to be initiated when the Kamitic mystery systems had been long extinct, I thought to myself and do I need to be initiated in the Kamitic mysteries?

That's when I learned that there are two types of formal initiations that exist. The most popular initiations are where an initiate goes through a step-by-step process where they die of their old ways and are supposed to be reborn, such as in baptism, marriage ceremonies like the Jumping of the Broom, etc. The second most popular formal initiation is initiation by recognition where the initiate must undergo a physical act before they are accepted by the greater whole, like circumcision, piercing, or some type of scarring like tattooing, as in rites of passage ceremonies. There is however, another type of initiation that is not commonly spoken of because most try to avoid it as much as possible. This informal initiation is not conducted by living people, but orchestrated by invisible hands and is referred to as "The Calling".

This type of initiation is commonly found amongst shamanic traditions around the world, because it is the oldest form initiation known to man. When one is "called" it is believe that they are being "called" by God, the ancestors or one's guardian spirits. The "Calling" is usually marked (but not always) by some extraordinary event surrounding the initiate's birth. The child may have been breached at birth or born with a caul covering their face. In some cultures peculiar moles and birthmarks are signs that the child has been "called". Other signs may be that the child displays an "odd behavior" (like a sixth sense, preferring solitude versus having company with others, etc.), which distance them from other children. The signs that one has been "called" are numerous and they vary from culture to culture. The one thing that all cultures that believe in a "Calling" type of initiation have in common, is that when an initiate has been called rather they know it or not. They will undergo an illness (either physical and/or psychological), which is will introduce the initiate to the inner mysteries, so that they can begin to fulfill their purpose. Then it hit me.

Contrary to popular belief, African Americans did retain their cultural ties to Africa, but it was syncretized or rather dissimulated with Protestant Christianity. Underneath the Eurocentric Christian mask lays the Kongo thinking of why many African Americans go to church, and a number of them do not. This philosophical thinking reveals itself in how African Americans interpret the biblical story *Jonah and the Whale*. Just like Jonah experienced a lot of obstacles because he refused to follow the Great Yahweh's will. In many African American churches when people experiences numerous problems, setbacks and a number of traumatic experiences. It is believed that they are being "Called" like Jonah, but the "Calling" does not just refer to being called to be a preacher or an evangelist. It is a call for a complete change of consciousness in one's actions, behaviors and manners, figuratively called *Baptized by Fire*. In other words, those who are serious and accept the teachings of Christ in their life are initiated into the metamorphosis. Those who have not accepted the teachings for whatever reason are seen as being uninitiated. It is this distinct African philosophy that takes Christianity and transforms it into a shamanic type initiation, thus making the Black Church an Afro – Atlantic religion.

But unfortunately, just like when Judaism took root amongst the Greeks and emerged into Christianity as it absorbed the Greek culture. And when Christianity settled among the Romans it adopted the oppressive Roman culture as it expanded across the globe with the aim of creating an empire. Many Afro – Atlantic religions due to a lack of African theology as in the case with the Black Christian Church, have adopted the Eurocentric cultural values that centers on money, resulting in them abandoning the original concepts and principles that they were established on. Although, I have nothing against making money, because everyone needs money in order to live as it is a necessity and requirement for living. Salvation nowadays has become big business! Unscrupulous individuals are charging astronomical prices just to be initiated into mystery systems designed to help people. Mega-churches are continuing to sprout up all over the United States and have begun to make their presence known in Latin America and Africa, but to maintain membership. These religious leaders refuse to stand up against injustice, refuse to speak against various societal deviations and perversions, which in essence is causing more problems than it solves.

The Purpose of the Kamitic Way

Iya had said while informing me that I was called to be a shaman that if I had been born in a traditional non-Western society, I would have been initiated by now. Papa told me something similar, that if I was younger and in Cuba I would be initiated as well. In fact, since I embarked upon this path, the subject of initiation has come up several times in various traditions, but the way was always closed. The reason I wasn't initiated into any formal tradition was because as Iya had once told me I needed to see everything, meaning I needed to understand the metaphysics and see how it applied. If I had undergone any formal initiation I would have most likely been indoctrinated with more dogmatic beliefs and ideas, thereby preventing me from fulfilling my destiny. This is why I was encouraged to walk the Kamitic Way.

It was this realization that made me to break from my Western trained – mindset and introduced me to the Kamitic mysteries. It was here I discovered that our universe is composed of dualities: light and dark, male and female, hot and cold, left and right, known and unknown. Meaning there are some things in this world we are meant to intellectually understand and some things that we are not going to understand or will remain a mystery. To guide us along the way, God creates archetypes (our ancestors, angels, guardian angels, spirits or whatever you prefer to call them) to assist us in our daily living. All of my experiences from the good to the bad were all part of my informal initiation. The numerous teachers that appeared in my times of need like Papa and Iya were the masters put in my life to show me the way. The entire experience helped me to discover the maa aankh (pronounced myaa – unk) and find my *la manera* or *maa* – personal way or truth.

What is the Maa Aankh?

Since the Kamitic philosophers left no texts (or none has been found), explaining the purpose of their spiritual traditions. Many scholars have painstakingly translated the Kamitic spiritual literature word for word, but they have not been successful in providing the public with practical information on how to use their translation. The reason is because the Kamitic spiritual texts – e.g. *Pert em Hru, the Coffin Texts, the Pyramid Texts,* etc. – were written for initiates in the Kamitic secret societies (commonly referred to as the Kamitic Mystery School to the uninitiated). In other words, although archeologists have been able to translate the Kamitic texts, they have not been able to decipher the secret code. This is the reason why to the uninitiated, the Kamitic spiritual texts appear to be books of magical spells, incantations and fanciful allusions.

Fortunately for our sake, knowing that the Kamitic philosophers were black and brown Africans, who had similar customs, practices, religious beliefs, and traditions as other traditional Africans in the continent, it becomes easy to decode the Kamitic literature by drawing comparisons with existing African cosmologies. This has already been done by several Kamitic inspired groups who have drawn one to one correspondences, between the Kamitic and various West African cultures (such as the Akan, Yoruba and Dahomean- Fon). I on the other hand was able to draw similarities between the Kamitic philosophy and the cosmology of the ancient Kongo by noting the similarities between the Kamitic and Kongo concepts like, Khepera and Kala, which are both

20

black in color and refer to the beginning, the start of something new and sunrise. Further investigations between these two cultures led me to find that before the Kongo was colonized. When an individual falls ill they might become a healer or priest specializing in healing others afflicted by the same illness they had previously survived. This was very similar to the initiatory practices of the Kamitic people and an example of a spiritual death/rebirth that occurs when one must purify them self of the negative elements acquired from dwelling in the physical world, influenced by Set.

I will be frank, I remember when I first made this discovery I still had doubts if what I had found was true. But when I had learned that a lawsuit in the pre-colonial Kongo was issued to an individual. The winner after being humiliated by the initial presentation of the lawsuit is purified by the tribunal's ruling. Then the winner may be adorned with white clay (or white cloth), symbolizing that they are innocent and have been exonerated. That's when I got my confirmation that this was a direct cultural link because Osar's colors were white as well, and his son Hru was wrongly accused but exonerated when he received the white crown, thus making the Pschent or Double Red and White Crown of Kamit. Rebirth I quickly realized pertained to balance or Maa and this is what led me to discover the maa aankh cosmogram, which according to my research is the foundation of the ancient Bantu of Kamit. As stated in my previous books, it is not known if the Kamitic people had a similar cosmogram. It is known based upon cultural similarities that they follow a similar model. This is possibly because all indigenous Africans created villages and city – states based upon some kind of cosmology in order to shape the people's identity.

The word "maa aankh" is composed of the Kamitic words maa meaning "balance, order, reciprocity, righteous, truth, etc." and aankh meaning "life" and "to swear an oath." The word maa aankh means:

1. The order of life.
2. To live holistically
3. To be in balance
4. To swear an oath to live righteously or truth.

The circle of the maa aankh moving in the counter clockwise direction symbolizes the movement of the sun. The four solar discs surrounding the diagram are the four moments of the sun: sunrise, midday, sunset and midnight. They represent the four stages that we as human beings follow,

21

which the ancient Bantu of Kamit noted. For instance, from right to left: when we awake we rise like the sun and the Kamitic philosophers called this moment Khepera (sunrise/birth). We become active and energetic during the midday, which was called Ra (midday/life). We retire or die like the setting sun, which corresponds to Ra Atum (sunset/death). Then we mysteriously must sleep so that we can do it all over again, similar to the moon at midnight, which the Kamitic philosophers found was similar to Amun Ra.

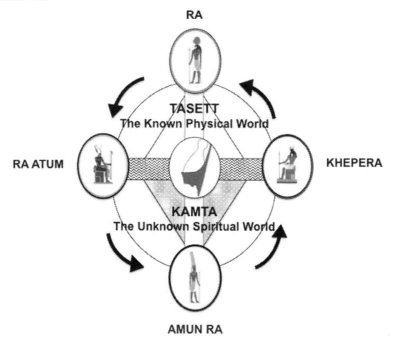

Maa Aankh Cosmogram

The upright triangle is TASETT – the Red Lands – is the known, physical, visible, material, ordinary, natural realm. TASETT also being the physical manifestation of the aggressive Shu is light, fire, masculinity, the desert, heat, the living world, etc. TASETT is hard, unyielding, active and noisy. While the inverted triangle KAMTA – "The Black Lands" – represents the invisible, spiritual, immaterial supernatural, extraordinary and unknown realm. KAMTA being the manifestation of passive Tefnut is darkness, water, femininity, the forest, cold, the land of the dead, etc. KAMTA is soft, gentle and everything that is within. It is also still and quiet. Therefore, there are two types of people: KAMTA (spiritual minded or civilized) and TASETT (wild and uncivilized).

These two great lands are joined together vertically by the Maa and separated by *nyun*, the great watery and chaotic abyss, which is the barrier and passageway, where Khepera rises in the land of the living and Ra Atum sets in the land of the dead. The *nyun* ensures that what is done in the past remains in the past, which is why most us do not have any recollection of the path that we chose prior to being born. The reason we pass through *nyun*, which washes away all memory of the life we will have, is obvious. If we had prior knowledge of the life we were going to live, most of us would not live and grow from the experience. If you knew from the beginning that you were going to be in a bad relationship, and out of the turmoil of that relationship you would have beautiful children that would grow up to be leaders. Would you still choose to be in that relationship? If you knew when you were going to die, how could you live your life while counting how many days you had left? This is why foreknowledge of the future is a major Catch-22 because you feel like you can't make any choices in life and are stuck with the decisions you have made. Thankfully because of the *nyun*, the living is given a chance to function in physical world with no inhibitions and the dead are given a chance to observe the past.

It was this unique observation that the ancient initiates initially imagined as being governed by Ra – the Visible Power (above) – that corresponded the midday sun and Set (the archetype of raw emotion, excessive passion, brute force, etc.). That led them to realize our life is governed by the choices we make symbolized as Hru (the archetype of freedom of will), while associating the bottom of the maa aankh with Amun Ra – the Hidden Power (below) – that corresponds to the left eye of Ra, the moon and Osar. Hence success in life depends upon one being able to stand on the edge of both lands, which means a contract or partnership must exist between the natural and the supernatural world, the physical and the spiritual realm, land of the living and the land of the dead, the living descendants – Hru – and the ancestral dead – Osar. This is the only way that the initiate could be successful and ever become born again or maa xheru[1] (pronounced maa – sharu or maa-tcheh-roo).

When I found my maa through the maa aankh, my health improved and my life increased drastically because now I knew what I was supposed to do. It was weird at first because it almost seemed like "good

---

[1] Maa xheru (also spelled maa kheru) literally means, "To be True of Voice" in other words, speak and live the truth. It also refers to rebirth.

luck" just fell out of the sky. I mean I got a better job, which led to better finances and everything. Now, I didn't stop having problems. Problems I quickly learned never go away and as long as we're living will never cease to exist. However, it became a lot easier to manage them, because understanding the maa aankh eliminated the constant anxiety, fear and worry associated with the future.

Kamta: The Heroic Spiritual Path

The purpose of sharing with you my personal experience is to help you to see that the reason I underwent so much was in part because I was suffering from a type of soul loss. Generally, soul loss is when part of the soul leaves to protect the individual from an abusive and/or traumatic experience. Due to misinformation about African traditions, many African Americans experienced a cultural soul loss when they ceased passing on their cultural traditions to succeeding generations in order to assimilate into the American way of life. As a result, the suffering individual grows up always searching and feeling disconnected from life, because they have cultural voids. Fortunately, there are numerous paths that were created by the Kamitic philosophers to deal with this problem. The most popular path or spiritual system that developed was outlined in the *Pert em Hru* (literally *The Book of Coming Forth by Day)*, but many contemporary practitioners have used it specifically for spiritual development. Thankfully, there were several other paths created and developed because the roots of Maa lie in ancient African shamanism. The path presented within these pages is called Kamta, named after the KAMTA region of the maa aankh, and it is a heroic path that focuses on every day, ordinary trials of life.

The difference between the spiritual development and heroic paths is that the latter is not overly concerned with spiritual enlightenment. Spiritual enlightenment is a by – product of a material goal. While spiritual enlightenment is a beautiful experience, it cannot put food on the table; help you pay your bills, etc. I have found that when our objectives are more goal-oriented, there's a better chance for greater result due to our own interests. For instance, when an individual on the spiritual development path meditates it is with the purpose of one day merging their consciousness with the Divine. Spiritual development from this perspective becomes more of a discipline and eventually a chore, like being told as a child to go to church without any objective at hand. You are just going out of tradition.

However, when an individual on the heroic path meditates or does any spiritual work, it is to get something done or to improve a physical situation like pay a bill, improve their relationship, increase their finances, heal the body, etc. Let me give you an example. I used to have a problem talking to my wife and her daughter. I didn't know what the problem was but I wanted to improve my relationship with them. So, since Nebhet is the patroness of relationships, I lit a candle and asked her for help in the matter. To assist me I made a commitment not to be so critical, cynical and sarcastic, but instead flattering and soothing. Four the next two days, I was reminded of the oath that I made to Nebhet, and later on the second day there was a breakthrough. My wife, her daughter and I were watching television and actually enjoying each other's company. We talked amongst ourselves and there was no problem at all. As soon as I noted the change, I made an offering to Nebhet as promised. It wasn't too long after that Nebhet showed me that the reason my relationship with my wife and daughter was estranged, was because I being the eldest son out of four boys (no sisters) didn't know how to achieve a balance with wife and her daughter on a personal level. I was use to talking to my brothers, male cousins, uncles and friends like guys talk, so we had to develop a tough rhinoceros skin that could deflect the criticism of naysayers. We also had to develop a sharp and witty response when someone talked about us, but I couldn't talk to girls and women like that all the time. They have a way of taking what you say in another direction. Since that time our relationship has gotten better, but it wasn't because I was focused on talking to women or not be too harsh. It was because my objective was to better the relationship between my wife, daughter and I.

As you can see, in the heroic path if spiritual enlightenment occurs that's great, but if it doesn't, that's great too. The reason is because the purpose of doing the spiritual work was not for spiritual enlightenment, but to accomplish a physical goal. The benefit of following the heroic path is that it does not require you to go off into some secluded place in order to learn it. You do not need an official or someone to reside over what you are doing. You do not need to adopt copy or mimic another's cultural practice and tradition. You do not need to wear a costume and you do not need to buy any special equipment, because it all takes place (for the most part) in the depths of your mind. This allows you to practice it anywhere and at any time, while you work, play, drive your car, etc.

Although you do not have to be initiated to practice Kamta, practicing it requires that you go through an informal self – initiation. This informal self – initiation follows the Rule of the Sun where one acknowledges where he or she is at in their life (in accordance to the maa aankh) and where they want to go. It is a natural process that we all must go through – birth, maturity, death and rebirth, but in the case of spiritual initiation. Spiritual death involves a change of consciousness from old behaviors and rebirth consists of the adoption of new behaviors, where one learns to be more social and spiritually responsible. This informal self – initiation begins at the death stage because any time we begin to have gross misfortunes, tragedies, numerous setbacks and obstacles, etc. (especially in regards to accomplishing a goal) like the prince Hru. It can be said that we are being defeated by Set and experiencing a spiritual death or a small death, who is metaphorically causing our sun to fall or set. In fact, anything that results in embarrassment, humiliation, suffering, shame, etc. is seen as a small death, which means that there is some impurity (destructive action, erroneous belief, incorrect behavior, wrong information, etc.) that has caused us to be defeated by Set.

Rebirth occurs by working with those on the other side to correct the errors of our ways and purify us of the stains of TASETT. You will know when you have been reborn because the signs of your small death and stains of TASETT (anger, despair, fear, guilt, resentment, shame, worry, etc.) in regards to your objective have been removed. In other words, the things you use to do, you will no longer do or engage in. You will suddenly see the errors of your ways. For most people change occurs, whenever we learn or see a new and better way of doing something. As you read in my previous example, it was by working with Nebhet in regards to my relationships I was spiritually reborn. Nebhet reminds me to be conscientious of my words especially when speaking to my wife and her daughter.

Every culture has their unique way of connecting to the Divine for obtaining healing, and this is an alternative form of healing that my ancestors developed to help me. With it, my plan is to heal, learn, share and prevent cultural soul loss by breathing new life in old traditions and creating new ones. Consequently, some of what you will find within these pages may disagree with other teachings, but this is not to say that what has been written here is absolute right and others are wrong. It is simply a different presentation of the same concepts and principles. As Papa once told me, "The only way to know if something is right for you is to try it out for yourself and see if it works. Never take anyone's word, because what works for them may not work for you."

Chapter 2:
The Kamitic Cosmology

Mention ancient Egypt to most people and what comes to mind are the pyramids, the sphinx and other great stone edifices that these ancient builders along the Nile River built. Further exploration will reveal that Ancient Egypt is an endless source of awe, inspiration and wonder to people all over the world, from all walks of life. Everyone from the astute archeologists to the aspiring artists and poets has been and continue to be inspired by the ancient Egyptians. Unfortunately, because no written texts have been found accurately explaining how these ancient people in Africa accomplished so many remarkable feats, without any of the advance technology we have today. A lot of theories have been proposed but many of these hypotheses are utter nonsense. To understand what I mean by nonsense, all one has to do is consider the theory that the founders of this great civilization were inspired by extraterrestrials or some other advance culture from a distant continent with an unknown origin.

The fact is that ancient Egypt is a civilization that was built in the interior of Africa (not the Middle East), but alongside the Nile River. The ancient Egyptians called their country KMT or Kamit, which means "black soil" and they called them selves Kamau – "people from the black lands." Although, filmmakers, historians and theologians claim that the Kamitic people had a number of cults and various religions. Contrary to popular belief, the Kamitic spiritual structure was a very simple system[2] based upon the belief in One Supreme God, whom was generically referred to as Netchar, which survives today as the word Nature.

The evolution of the Kamitic culture began with them observing nature and the relationship the living had with the dead. Just like people nowadays wonder about what happens after death, the Kamitic people did the same thing. What they discovered was that everything that is alive will eventually see death. Death occurred whenever an individual ceased to inhale and exhale breath. This meant that life was associated with breathing and death was signified by the absence of breath.

---

[2] It was the simplicity of the Kamitic spiritual tradition and the *Story of Osar* that caused early Christian writers to borrow numerous concepts from it, which can still be seen today.

Since all living things including human beings from different backgrounds and varying beliefs all shared the same air. It was determined that the Almighty God was not bias and did not favor any man or woman over another. God instead was a just and merciful Supreme Being that governed everything that existed; hence they called the Almighty God, Nebertcher – the Lord of Everything – The Supreme Being.

The pre-dynastic Kamitic people understood however that human beings were uniquely different from all of the other creatures on the planet. One of the most significant differences that were cited between animals and human beings was that unlike animals that abandon their dead to the climate or ravenous beasts of the earth. Human beings after abandoning their dead seemed to sense that there was something after death, and that the recently deceased although not physically alive had survived death. It was this curious observation that inspired them to choose to remember their dead by burying them.

Although, no one actually knows what these ancient philosophers were truly thinking. Based upon recovered artifacts, we can imagine that these pre-dynastic shamans first began experimenting with breathing since breath was associated with life. Through their experimentation they discovered how to enter into trance and proficiency with this state of awareness allowed them to enter the mystical world of dreams. It was here they met their deceased loved ones and first became aware that the soul does not die after death.

In time as they continued to see the souls of loved ones in their dreams and began to receive instructions from them, it was understood that the soul of the recently deceased retained his or her personality, character traits, prejudices, etc. as they had in life. So, began the mysterious customs associated with burying the dead, in order to prevent angering them. Again, this is only speculation, but one can imagine that as these ancient dwellers continued to explorer the mysteries of the mind – spirit. They came across some departed souls that were not at peace and had died in a horrible manner, because of the life that they lived. This led them to determine that the choices that we make are what determine our existence in the afterlife and not God. It was then concluded that if it is the choices that we make that determine our afterlife, and it is the choices that we make that distinguishes us from animals. Then human beings choose to be here, which means every child is a soul reborn. Inspired by

28

nature and their observation of death, this led the Kamitic people to theorize how the universe was created.

Mapping the Kamitic Universe

Every culture has at least one theory on how the universe was created but the Kamitic people, throughout their long history, had several creation theories. The reason is because their models were not just used to explain the origin of the universe. The purpose of creating cosmologies is to explain how everything from the universe to the human mind functions. It is a blueprint for understanding everything, especially energy in order to create a physical change from a spiritual reality. This is what made the Kamitic philosophy extremely flexible and pragmatic, because unlike a lot of Western philosophies that focus on proving if something is scientifically correct. The Kamitic philosophy was not about which philosophy was right or wrong, rather it focused upon what was ideal and most importantly what worked. Unlike Westerners who condemn and persecute Catholics and others for using ritual aids, non-Westerners simply accepted it as it being part of that individual's truth, their maa. In Kamit, if something worked for one individual they were encouraged to use it, but if it didn't work they were encourage to use another.

This is why the best way to understand Kamitic philosophy is by approaching the Kamitic literature from a humble, imaginative, playful and metaphorical perspective. Then, understanding that the various animal and other symbols were not used to explain nature, but instead express a set of beliefs. In fact, all of the Kamitic spiritual texts use a host of animals (and other symbols) metaphorically to express the essence of these things. For instance, a hippopotamus (depending upon its use) would be considered a dangerous enemy because this wild beast would hide under the water and attack a passerby in its boat. This same image could easily be used to symbolize any enemy, such as an assailant waiting in the corners or the sudden outburst of an emotion leading to a chaotic outcome. Therefore, emotional instability or acting like a hippopotamus from the Kamitic perspective was seen as acting heated or being impulsive, which was not ideal. The ideal way to conduct one's affairs according to the Kamitic perspective was to be reserved in speech, silent and think before acting. As you can see, when you read the Kamitic literature from this perspective. All of the so-called Kamitic cults appear to be different schools of thought dedicated to the study of the "Right

Way" to act, behave, conduct one's affairs, etc. or the Maa. As you can imagine there was a school dedicated to studying dance, martial arts, military strategy, political philosophy, etc.

In general, the Kamitic creation theory states that in the beginning there was nothing that existed except for a great cosmic void called *nyun*, which was filled with fundamental Hidden Ra Energy or Amun Ra.

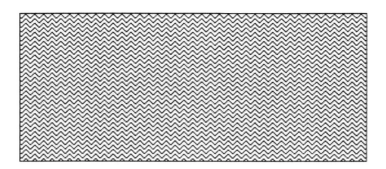

Then the Almighty God, Nebertcher spoke and caused Ra – the Visible Energy – to emerge from the darkness. Afterwards the Almighty God, Nebertcher spoke and caused Ra – The Visible Energy to come into existence.

Finding no place for Ra to stand, the Almighty God, Nebertcher called Maa to ascend out of the *nyun*, and through Maa balance, law, order, truth and true love was established and became the foundation our universe was built upon.

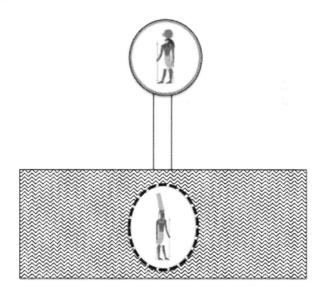

The ascension of Maa caused the hot, masculine, upward principle called shu and the cool, feminine, downward principle called tefnut, (the complimentary opposites or Kamitic yang and yin) to also come into existence. Thus duality is balance, law, order, truth and true love, which is Maa.

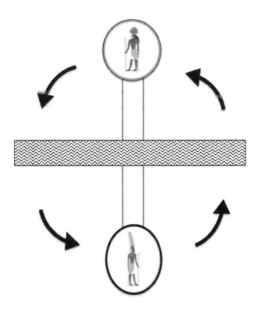

Together shu and tefnut brought the many dualities – e.g. light and dark, high and low, hot and cold, fire and water, air and earth, male and female – into our universe respectively. Shu and tefnut are interdependent upon each other; as a result one cannot exist without the other.

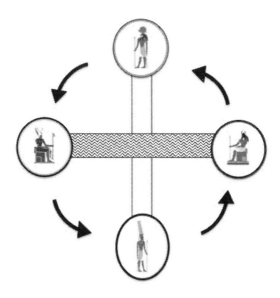

These complementary forces caused the Ra to become KhepeRa (the Creative Energy Force/Consciousness), Ra Atum (the Completed Energy/Consciousness or Transformative Energy/Consciousness that was "born in *nyun* but out of it"). Eventually, matter was formed and the birth of the universe took place.

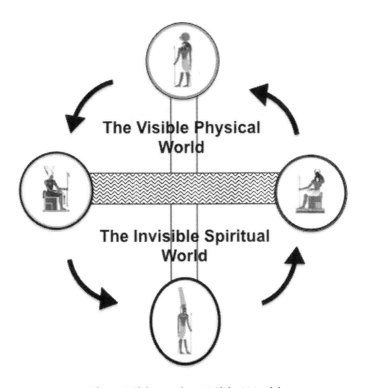

The Visible and Invisible World

As you can see, Ra is not the sun, which is "atum" in the Kamitic language, but is the primordial creative and generative energy associated with consciousness symbolized as the sun. For instance, we say today that when someone has a lot of intelligence that they are bright, which is not speaking about their intellect but their being. The Kamitic people thought in a similar manner and when speaking to each other. They knew the difference because of the way the word Ra was pronounced. It is difficult for us to do this because most people do not know the Kamitic language. There were many interpretations of the word "ra" so, to distinguish between them all. Rau (Ra spelled with a "u") is used when referring to the primordial creative and generative power of the sun, the life force, and Chi energy, or the Spirit of God. Ra (and all its uses of it without the "u")

33

is used to refer to states of consciousness symbolized by the movements of the sun.

It is Ra Atum that completes the creation process by separating the heavens from the earth, the physical from the spiritual, and everything in between. Due to the Maa and the influences of shu and tefnut, and time and space, Amun Ra, Khepera, Ra, and Ra Atum, the Rau was stirred and everything began to take its place in the *nyun*, thus causing the stars, planets and galaxies to take their respective places in space. This is how our universe and the numerous universes that exist began to take form. The whole process for everything that exists and will exists from the creation of universes to every biological life form repeats itself beginning with Amun Ra. Together these forces acting as interdependent parts in a whole balance the Rau and create the "order of life" or maa aankh.

Therefore, according to the maa aankh (pronounced maa' unkh), since our universe initially was in a state of chaos and physically came into existence, by emerging out of the invisible realm in order for Maa to exist. Everything that exists or will come into existence initially exists in a chaotic state and seeks to establish balance, harmony or Maa in order, for the God Force to move constructively and create life. In other words, everything has an invisible spiritual nature and a visible physical aspect to itself including human beings. Everyone and everything has a maa aankh.

Chapter 3:
The Cosmology of the Soul

Have you ever asked yourself what makes human beings different from animals? Why according to most religious texts, are human beings placed a step above the creatures of the earth and even a step above all of the angelic beings?[3] According to Kamitic philosophy everything that exist was created by the Almighty God Nebertcher, which means everything is sacred but the difference between animals and human beings is that the former acts and behaves instinctively; whereas the latter has the ability to rise above their instincts. It was this understanding that led the Kamitic philosophers to conclude that just like the human body was a complex organism consisting of several organs acting as independent parts of a whole. We technically speaking are all spirits consisting of several spiritual divisions. In order to understand what makes us unique amongst all of creation we need to understand how our spiritual organs function within our being.

The Spiritual Anatomy of Man & Woman

The spiritual anatomy of every living being is very complex system composed of several divisions, which act in a similar manner.[4] For instance, just like the physical brain is the organ that keeps everything within the body functioning smoothly. It is believed that there exists a spiritual brain that ensures that everything within our being is functioning smoothly as well from a spiritual perspective. The spiritual brain or head was referred to as the *ba*, which governed an individual's destiny, purpose

---

[3] In Psalm 8:4-5 we find that human beings weren't created to be beneath angels, but beneath God. Sloppy scholarship led the translators of the King James Bible to translate the Hebraic word *elohim* to angels, when it should be translated as God.

[4] In some spiritual systems it was believed there were seven or nine divisions while others believed there were 14. Again, the Kamitic philosophers were not bound by religious dogma and they didn't concern themselves with what was right or wrong based upon an intellectual measuring stick. They backed whichever system was the most effective and practical. If the spiritual system with 14 divisions worked for an individual then that's the one they used, but if not they adapted to that system. This system is based upon the nine divisions of the spirit.

in life and therefore is what gave an individual the life to live (*shekhem*, *khu*, and the *ren*). The *ba* was therefore the breath of life or the divine spark, divine consciousness or upper spirit.

Just like everything that physically exists is a mirror reflection of what exists spiritually, the division of the spirit that controls the *khab* (the physical body), *khabit* (instincts), and *ka* (personality/personal power), was called the *sahu*. The *sahu* is the spiritual vehicle, physical body consciousness or lower spirit. But what makes everything that exists different is the soul, which is what the Kamitic philosophers called the *ab*.

Everything that physically exists has a *ba*, which gives it the ability to live and exist, and a *sahu*, which provides every being with a physical shell or vehicle[5]. Since, human beings are the only living organisms that have managed to evolve their *ab* to the spiritual level at the Ra Atum moment. Generally speaking it is said that only human beings are the only ones that have an *ab*. All life forms sense the inevitable end that we call death at the Ra Atum moment, but only human beings. Sense that there is something beyond the veil, which we commonly refer to as the afterlife. It is this human characteristic that makes us perform some sort of rite so that the dead will rest in peace.

All of the great spiritual traditions begin with this universal concept of Death and Rebirth, because this is what marks the beginning of our evolution. It is what distinguishes human beings from all of the other living beings on the planet. For instance, most people choose to do what is good versus evil in hopes of going to a better place when they die, but human beings are still in the dawn of their spiritual evolution. This explains the reason why people choose to do what is right or good out of fear. In all honesty, no one should have to threaten people with the idea that they will go to hell or burn in a place of eternity if they truly understood what righteousness is all about. The fact that religious leaders have to resort to such means is a clear sign that most people do not understand the nature of their being or what spirituality and righteous living truly means. Therefore, to move beyond this point we need to truly understand the nature of our spiritual anatomy or understand our divinity. We need to understand why we were created *in the image of God* instead of

---

[5] Technically speaking everything also has an *ab* but the *ab* of plants is in a vegetative state at the Khepera moment and the *ab* of animals is primarily still instinctual at the Ra moment.

just glossing over the concept because it conflicts with our dogma. This is why out of convenience I have subdivided the nine divisions into three parts – the *ba*, *sahu* and *ab*.

The Ba – The Divine Consciousness or Upper Spirit

Our *ba* is what connects us back to the Divine. It is what is commonly referred to as our *spirit* (even though technically speaking all of the division are our spirit), but it is not God – the Supreme Being. The *ba* – the divine spark, gives everything that physically exist purpose, because it is our spiritual intuition. It is the divine Light of God, that exists in every living being and connects us will all the living things. The *ba* is responsible for our destiny and everything we are supposed to learn in our lifetime in order to achieve our purpose. It enters into our body the moment we took our first breath and brought with it the divine life force, essence of God, intuition, wisdom, spiritual prowess, dreams, and memories of the past, our destiny and all the things we need to survive spiritually. It corresponds to Jung's collective unconscious.

The *ba* never truly abandons us or leads us astray. It is always near. It is what guides us from birth and will remain with us until we die, because it is our personal guardian angel. Upon death, the *ba* returns back to God where it awaits to be reborn, so it can help us fulfill our destiny. It is our *ba* that determines the life that we live prior to returning to the land of the living. Our *ba* determines who our family will be, our ethnicity, sex, race, religion, the problems we will have in life and what we need to learn or accomplish in our lifetime. Our *ba* is essential to our happiness because it know all of our needs and wants. In fact, nothing occurs in our life that our *ba* is not aware of, which means that it is our *ba* that whispers in our ear and speaks from within in our times of despair. A lot of time we may not hear our *ba* because of all the mental chatter. Fortunately, our *ba* never abandons us and is always near, imagined perched on our crown or shoulders. It is always waiting for us to reconnect with it by going within, so that it can take our prayers and other request to the Divine. In the near future we will see that our *ba* is what gives us the ability to co – create and change. It is what makes miracles (or magic, whichever you prefer to call it) possible.

The Sahu: The Physical Consciousness, Lower Spirit or Flesh

Since our *ba* derives what it knows from the Divine, which gives our *ba* unlimited freedom. Because the Maa establishes balance and harmony throughout the universe, the polar opposite of the *ba* is our *sahu*. The *sahu* is what gives everything that exist the ability to express its *ba*, hence divine purpose.

The purpose of the *sahu* is to assist all living beings in physically surviving on the planet. It governs as stated earlier all of our bodily functions by relying upon our genetic and learned memories. Through genetic or ancestral memories (DNA), the *sahu* uses these memories to influence the shape, height, width and function of our body. The reason you look like a distant relative or walk like your grandfather, is because all of these memories are stored on a cellular level. Learned memories are those memories we have acquired from our family, friends, school, church, the media, etc. All of these memories are stored in various muscles of our body and categorized as good or bad memories based upon our pleasurable or painful experience. So whenever we feel a pulsing, sharp, tightening of our muscles, it is a warning sign from our *sahu* that there is imminent or impending danger near. Whenever our muscles are relaxed, restful and soothing, it is a message from our *sahu* that we are feeling something pleasurable. This is how our *sahu* uses our emotions to store our learned memories and alert us when we are doing something that is pleasurable or painful. Using these emotions our *sahu* stimulates our most innate desires and needs, which according to Abraham Maslow's '*Hierarchy Of Needs*' in ascending order of significance are:

1. Self- actualization Needs: the need for self – fulfillment, creativity, morality and ability to solve problems
2. Esteem Needs: self – achievement, confidence, respect for and by others
3. Social Needs: acceptance, affection, intimacy and love
4. Safety Needs: protection from physical, natural, material, financial, economical, and emotional harm
5. Physiological Needs: food, water, shelter, sleep, air, sex, etc.

Therefore, what this means is that if the needs of the *sahu* aren't met then it will create problems in our life, because unlike the *ba*, the *sahu* is very temperamental and impressionable. It corresponds to Freud's Id or the 'child' part of our mind. Even though it is extremely logical, it lacks the ability to rationalize and distinguish right from wrong, left from right, past from present, and so on. This is why children have to be taught what appropriate and inappropriate behavior is.

The *sahu* is very logical. This is why it interprets everything that it hears, sees, smells, feels and tastes literally, which it stores in its memories. It categorizes all of our memories as either pain or pleasure, and naturally prefers pleasure to pain. Pleasure is the sign that the body is relaxed and pain is the sign that the body is stressed or tensed. This is the reason we all prefer to do certain things instead of others. It is the same reason why when it comes to doing chores or things that we know we need to do, we usually procrastinate. Whereas things we enjoy doing like our hobbies we have no problem doing. It is because our *sahu* typically is lazy and does not like change. It tries its best to avoid anything that it considers to be painful by moving us towards the things we enjoy and like.

What this means is that all of our experiences have been categorized as pleasurable or painful, and it is these experiences that our *sahu* uses to influence our actions and behaviors. For instance, if you ever felt rejection, your *sahu* would have motivated you to act in a certain way to avoid ever experiencing that feeling again. If corrective measures are made you would become shy, feel uncomfortable, etc. and would find comfort in standing alongside a wall, in the corner or somewhere when interacting with large groups or being in unfamiliar places. While this behavior would appear too antisocial and clearly would not help in advancing your career, your *sahu* would see it as being better than being rejected. It gets worst.

If you are working at a job you don't like, in a relationship that seems unproductive or involved in anything that you find to be unpleasant. Over time your *sahu* would get tired and look for ways to resolve the issue itself by responding to the stressful situation in its own manner. Again, its inability to reason would cause it to look for the least painful solution to the dilemma you are in. Your *sahu* may cause you to become ill at your job. In a relationship you may begin to have headaches or some other body aches or viral infection. These are solutions that your *sahu* would see as being more pleasurable then being in the present situation because you are avoiding something that is painful. Unless it is firmly expressed to your *sahu* the reason for experiencing the discomfort, such as exercising to get a better physique, studying to get an "A" on an exam, facing rejection in order to become a better salesperson, etc.

Funny thing as I write this I had to attend an engagement that I wasn't looking forward to attending, because of previous experience. This event that was supposed to be festive usually ended on a sour note. You know those types of events where people drink too much, lose self – control, get loose lips, get false pride, say whatever they want, and the next thing you know there's an altercation, which was all created by Set, the Kamitic spirit of chaos and confusion whom you will meet later on. Anyway, it was hard for me to relax and enjoy myself. My *sahu* was tensed and would have been perfectly okay with staying home and relaxing or, being with real friends in environment that I controlled. Unfortunately, it was not my party and the people there were not my friends and didn't share any interest. I felt out of place, tensed and even though I tried not to appear to be antisocial, I was ready to go because my *sahu* was not comfortable in this environment. If it were a child, I would hear my *sahu* saying, "I hate it here. I am ready to go. Tell me again, why are we here?" It wasn't long afterwards I got a throbbing headache, which I knew my *sahu* was responsible for. It created an excuse for me to leave the event and it explained my actions and behaviors. It is far easier to tell someone, "I apologize, I just have a headache" then it is to say, "Your party is horrible, because the people here are jerks that cannot control how much alcohol they drink!"

Our *sahu* not knowing any better does what it must to avoid pain. It is our natural way of responding to unfamiliar and stressful events and situations, whether they are tangible or intangible. Think of an animal sensing danger and developing a defensive reaction to avoid its adversary and you will get a hint at how your *sahu* functions. For instance, the *sahu* of some animals secretes a strong offensive odor whenever it feels threatened. Porcupines defend themselves from predators with their quills. Our *sahu* defends us the same way by creating similar physiological responses when we feel threatened or stressed.

Stress, while we are on the subject, is the natural way of doing things. Everything that we do from chewing our food, to breathing, walking, etc. involves us using stress. Stress is necessary in order for us to live. It is through stress that we develop our muscles, but in order for our muscles to develop they have to relax in order to recuperate. The natural cycle of things is that we move from a relax state to a stressful state and

40

back to a relax state. If stress continues to build and there is no period of relaxation where healing (recuperation) can occur, discomfort sets in which gives way to illness, disease, etc. On the flipside, if there is too much relaxation and no stress at all. We will feel aches, pains, lethargic and sluggish as if we have slept too long. What this means is that anything that is done for too long or for an extended period of time will cause our *sahu* discomfort. This includes (but is not limited to) anger, anxiety, fear, worry, etc. as well as negative criticism and negative words like being called stupid, lazy, a clodhopper, fool, idiot, etc, which will result in it responding in a negative manner.

What this means (and I will reiterate this again throughout the book) if you want to create a change in your life. You have to strongly impress it upon your *sahu*, so that it remembers what you want. When I say strongly I mean it has to be so emotionally stimulating that it becomes a permanent fixture in your mind. Like, the reason you will not put your hand on a hot stove is because your *sahu* remembers it will burns. Everything we do out of habit is based upon some memory that is tied to some emotional response, so to impress our *sahu* we have to follow this same procedure to get what we want.

Understand. Your *sahu* functions perfectly by Divine design. A prime example of this can be seen by observing how healing of a wound occurs. If you detach yourself from your wound, you will see that all wounds are psychosomatic and that the pain is your body's way of activating the healing properties of the body. Note that if it is a laceration, the bleeding, swelling and warmth associated with the wound, is the body's way of defended itself against infection. Soon a scab will form regardless if you put any ointment on the wound or not. All of this takes place without you telling it to do so, because this is what the *sahu* was designed to do. What deter this natural process are the various influences like negative imagery, criticism, etc. that bombard your *sahu*. Combine this with the *sahu's* inability to reason and you have a potent mixture on your hand.

Your *sahu* therefore needs constant encouragement and reinforced with positive actions, behaviors, affirmations and declaration. Even though we are born with a *ba* we must learn right from wrong, the difference between appropriate and inappropriate behavior and so on. This is accomplished through our *ab*.

41

The Ab – The Spiritual Heart, the Human Soul

The *ab* as previously mentioned corresponds to our rational conscious mind and our will, which gives us the freedom to make choices in life. It is the "Me, Myself and I" part of our being. When we make a decision to do something we also make a decision not to do other things. We make a choice to follow what is "true to our heart." This means that we are not obligated to do anything we don't want to. This is why the *ab* is called our "spiritual heart" or the human soul.

Our *ab* is primal, authentic, and free from the emotional attachments of the world. It is because of our *ab*, it is natural for us to look for ways to improve the quality of life for all. It is our *ab* that wants the best out of life, wants to be healthy, successful, have abundance and be rich. These are all natural wants of the *ab*, which desires to be free.

It is our *ab* that drives us to want to understand the universe and gives us the yearning to perfect our soul. It is also what gives us the ability to express ourselves from a spiritual perspective. For instance, it is because of our *ab*, we as human beings don't abandon our dead to the elements or ravenous beasts in nature, but instead performs some type of rite wishing our deceased loved ones peace in the hereafter. Although, we may not have scientific proof of the existence of an afterlife, something tells us that this physical life is not final. That something, which speaks from our gut or solar – plexus and provides us with extrasensory perception is our *ab*.

It is because of our *ab*, unlike animals that must rely on their instincts in order to survive, we as human beings can choose to rely upon the instincts of our *sahu* or upon the divine nature of our *ba* to resolve our problems but understand. Most of the unwise decisions and mistakes that we make in life are due to us not having our *ab* directly connected to our *ba*. All of us have made some choices and decisions that we have regretted making and if given a chance. We wish we could go back and correct those errors. All of these problems occurred because our *ab* seeking to express its freedom made choices and decisions without receiving proper guidance from our *ba*. Our *ba* remember, reveals to us that we are all connected to one another. As a result, our actions and behaviors will have a ripple effect on everyone regardless if we are aware of it or not. It is only when our *ab* is directly connected to our *ba* we can see the impact we have upon others regardless if they are our family members, friends, neighbors, coworkers, the lady at the grocery store, the clerk at the movies, whoever. We therefore, have to strengthen our *ab's* ability to focus on our *ba*, which is strengthens our will to ignore the influence of our *sahu*. But what really is "Will?"

Well, basically your "will" is your ability to concentrate or focus on making a decision. For instance, if you go to the supermarket for a few apples and you come out with a lot of items that you didn't even need. Your will is not very strong. A strong will is about sticking to what you want. You want a few apples, so you go to the store; ignore all of the advertisements, sale pitches, etc. and go straight to the produce section. You get your apples and ignore all of the tabloid mess while waiting in line and you come out with your apples. Although this may sound very trivial, it is extremely difficult for a number of people to actual do. As you can imagine, if it is difficult to focus on getting a few produce, then what about when it comes to more important matters like furthering your education, focusing on a diet, managing your temper, being faithful in a relationship with others (both personal and impersonal), etc. So, you see we have a lot of freedom and with this freedom come the responsibility to develop and strengthen our *ab*.

As you can see, our *ab* technically speaking is the only thing within our being that we can control. It can be said that the reason God gives human beings an *ab* is so that we can be God's eyes, ears, mouth and hands in the world of the living. When we become aware, that's when God becomes aware and is able to implement change, which creates a ripple effect throughout the world. When we sense that there is a problem, God senses there is a problem and can provide us with a solution as to how to resolve the dilemma. God basically lives and experiences life by living through us. It is God that wants to enjoy life, create inventions, be successful, play music, succeed in business, etc. and in order to accomplish these goals (your goals). God must do it through you. Man and woman therefore, are supposed to be the physical representation or stewards of God on earth, hence the purpose of being godlike, Christ-like, Buddha-like, etc., but God will not force you to accept the Divine as your guide. You have to choose to allow God through your *ba* to be your guide.

In other words, no one can make you do better but your "self" or *ab*. If you are down and out, it is because you have chosen to be down out or have simply given up. But, the day you decide "enough is enough" and you get "tired of being tired" that is when you stir the wheels of change. This is when you *ba* takes notice and sets out to assist you because you have willed it so. Your *ab* is intimately connected to your *ba*, but your *ba* will only assist when you choose to connect to it.

Spirituality Made Simple and Plain

If everything that God created is given a *ba* and a *sahu* including animals, plants, trees, the forces of nature, rocks, minerals, places in nature like the seas, mountains, etc. However, man and woman are the only beings on the planet that have advanced their *ab*, which gives us the freedom to do whatsoever we will while living on the planet. Since the *sahu* is limited and our *ba* is unlimited. Spirituality simply put is about connecting to our higher spirit, inner self, the indwelling intelligence, our personal guardian angel or our *ba* in order to improve the quality of our life.

This means that if you are living according to the belief that you are going to do good in order to go to heaven and keep from going to hell. You are living way beyond your spiritual potential, because your *ba* gives you the ability to do so much more. If you were to just learn how to work with your *ba* the fate of your afterlife would take care of itself. It is sort of like, if you focus upon going to college you don't have to worry about high school because it is a given that you are going to graduate from the latter in order to get into college. We just have to trust our *ba*.

It can't be overstated that our *ba* knows everything about us. It knows our strengths and our weaknesses, even when we do not choose to admit them to ourselves. Our *ba* knows what we like and we do not like. It knows our talents and what we are good at. It knows what we have mastered and what we need to work on. It knows what we do not want and what we want before we even ask. It also knows what will inspire us and what will discourage us. It also knows who it needs to connect to in order to inspire us to move, because it is the most intimate part of our being. Therefore, when we do not follow our *ba* and listen to it speaking deep from within or whispering in our ear. We feel defeated and we beat our self-up emotionally. The reason is because our *ba* is constantly trying to inspire us to be better than what we were. Our *ba* wants us to have a good life, be happy, have money and all of our needs provided for, but it wants most importantly for us to fulfill our destiny, which is to grow spiritually. In other words, our *ba* helps us to overcome our anger, anxiety, fears, guilt, worries, etc. Let me give you an example.

44

Not too long ago as I was writing about this a job opening came up. I learned about the job from my supervisor who suggested that I apply for this position, which was all prompted by my *ba*, because the *ba* is connected to everyone. Now, I knew I had the training to do the job but I had a little doubt on if I was qualified, which was coming from my *sahu*. I decided with my *ab*, to apply for the job and if it was meant to be I would get it, right? So, I applied and sure enough out of the seven people on the interview committee, six of them I had a working relationship with. When I interviewed with them, it was the best interview I ever had, ending with everyone laughing. I mean it was a sure thing. I felt sorry for the other candidates because I knew their interview couldn't be any better than mine. The following week, I was offered the job, which paid almost 20% more than my current position. Wait, it gets better. Right after I decided to take the position, I discovered that my current position was being phased out.

As you can see, if I had followed the doubt based upon fear presented by my *sahu* I would have most likely been out of a job and on an unemployment line. This meant that *ba* saw in advance the future. My *ba* tapped my supervisor on the shoulder, who made the suggestion that I apply for the job. All I had to do was make a decision to either follow my *sahu* or my *ba*, and thankfully, I chose the latter.

This taught me a very valuable lesson about my *ba* and *sahu*, which is that our *ba* always speaks to us. The problem is that many of us simply choose not to follow the inspiration and intuitions of our *ba*, and usually this is because, we think that when a person listens to their *ba* or inner voices that they are insane. Thankfully, this attitude is beginning to change due to the numerous artists, musicians, educators, successful businessperson, inventors, mathematicians, scientists, etc. that have testified to the fact that by following their masterful and wise *ba*. They were able to achieve greatness and achieve their dreams. This is due to the fact that our *ba* connects us directly to the Divine.

It has to be remembered that our *sahu* draws its inspiration from TASETT – the physical realm and our limited earthly experiences, so every time you feel anxiety, fear, guilt, worry, etc. these are all based upon experiences from the past. The *ba* draws from the KAMTA – the unlimited spiritual realm, which is omnipotent, omnipresent and

45

omniscient. This gives our *ba* unlimited ability and access to do anything that is physically impossible.

Now understand, our *sahu* does not deliberately sabotage us and keeps us from accomplishing our dreams, it does this by default. This is because its purpose is to help us to physically survive and in order for it to accomplish its objective. Our *sahu* seeks to understand the physical world around us, but in doing so it prevents our *ba* from working on the objective at hand.

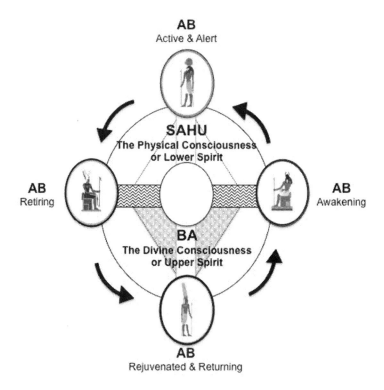

Cosmology of the Soul

The trick to working with your *ba* is that when you hand a problem over to it to work upon, as you saw in the previous example. You have to totally ignore the influences that come from your *sahu*. You cannot think or worry about it, because this will cause whatever your *ba* is working on to enter into your *sahu* awareness. For instance, if I had begun thinking, "What if I am not qualified?" or "I wonder how this is going to work out?" All of these questions would have prompted my *sahu* to devise of a way to make something happen, which would have led to a complete shamble. Resulting in my sulking, sucking my teeth and being upset with the world, when the real problem is that I should have followed my *ba* and not my *sahu*.

Our *ba* knowing all of our strengths and weakness will not present us with something that we are not fully capable of doing. Nor will it put us in a situation that we cannot handle. As a matter of fact, while we're on the subject, your *ba* does not instruct you to harm others[6]. It inspires you to reach your highest good by working with others. It inspires you to overcome your shortcomings, but what we have to learn how to do is to learn how to listen to it. However, there is another reason for following our *ba*.

Reincarnation of the Human Soul

Since we have established that our *sahu* division governs our physical body, our *ab* governs our soul or spiritual heart and our *ba* is our divine consciousness. When our physical body dies and has exhaled its last breath, the *ba* exits the body and returns to the Divine. The *sahu* consciousness (along with the body) returns to the earthly realm to provide another body for another soul, but because the *ab* is a division of the spirit, which makes it immortal. The *ab* of a deceased simply exists in the spiritual realm. Keeping in mind that our *ab* seeks to improve or better itself, by connecting with our *ba*. It lingers around until it can once again join with the *ba*, where it will receive a new objective or new destiny and reincarnate back to the land of the living in order to continue its development towards perfection.

Although this may seem like a complex concept to understand, if we abandon the erroneous belief that the only reason we are born is to praise and worship God, so that we can die and either go to heaven or hell, and look at this from a reasonable perspective. We have to see that surely Nebertcher would have a more intelligent plan in mind. If you

---

[6] There are a number of people who have claimed that their guardian spirit was inspiring them to act from saintly individuals like Joan of Arc to homicidal maniacs like the Son of Sam. Clearly, when compare this to the maa aankh we can see that individuals that claim be doing some deity's work are following their lower nature. Only the *sahu* thinks about self-preservations by harming others because it is animalistic.

think about how we are all created by the Divine, which means we are a microcosm of a greater Macrocosm and everything that occurs within us occurs in the Universe on a minute scale. We are all spirits within a physical body. It makes perfect sense that the reason we were physically created is to master the physical realm. In other words, the only way for a spiritual being to experience the physical realm and evolve is to be born into the physical realm. Without a physical body we cannot experience the physical world, but to remind us of our divinity we are given a *ba*.

So we have to incarnate into the physical world because this is the only way our *ab* can evolve. The purpose of physical hardships is so that we can learn how to connect with our *ba* and overcome these adversities. This means the more we incarnate into the physical world. The more we learn how to master the physical plane. Eventually, after so many incarnations our *ab* would have evolved to the point that we do not need to incarnate into the world of the living. This occurs when we have totally transcended our ego as Jesus had done. Then we can finally return back to the Source or Nebertcher's Rau. It is only by following our *ba* that this phenomenon is made possible.

Communicating With Your Personal Guardian Angel

It is important that we develop an intimate relationship with our *ba*, which acts as our personal guardian angel. Although, many traditions may claim that getting in touch with your inner self or your personal guardian angel is a very long, laborious task requiring a lot of self –discipline, it is actually a very easy thing to do. There are several ways to get in touch with your *ba*, but the easiest is to introvert our *ab* awareness.

When we are wide-awake and our awareness is focused on everything outside of our being. Our *ab* is said to be at the Beta state of awareness because it is extroverted. When we draw our awareness within like when we daydream, fall asleep or just awake from sleep, we are in the Alpha state of awareness. This is also called Twilight or entering into trance. It is in this state of awareness that we can easily communicate with our *ba*.

One of the easiest ways I have found is to just sit comfortably in a straight back chair and close your eyes. Take a few deep breaths and allow your body to relax. Let all of the thoughts and ideas that come to your mind pass through by not focusing on them at all. Meaning if an idea comes to your mind like, "What's for dinner?" Ignore it. Try your best not to think about anything. Just relax. If however, you find yourself dwelling or thinking about an idea that comes to mind. Don't beat yourself up about it. Once you catch yourself simply stop thinking about it and relax. Eventually you will feel like your body is swaying or having energy sensations pass through it. Your body may feel like it is cold or

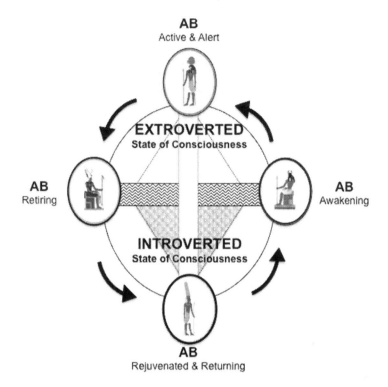

Introverted & Extroverted Consciousness

hot, or you may have some other type of physical sensation. These are all signs from your *sahu* that you have crossed the threshold and are in direct communication with your *ba*. At this time you can thank your *ba* for all of the good things that you have in life. You just simply say, "Thank you for _____." If you prefer something more traditional that will help you to focus, as I do at times. You may light a little white birthday candle to your *ba* and express your gratitude. To light a candle for positive influence, light the wick first, then light the base of the candle and firmly put it in its place. When you have finished you can end your prayer by saying, "Amen" which is Kamitic for "So be it."

Proficiency in the above technique allows you to communicate with your *ba* anywhere and everywhere. You don't necessarily have to sit down to do it either, so long as you relax and recognize the signs that you are in direct communication with your *ba* will be expressed by your *sahu* (energy sensations, hot and cold sensations, rocking or swaying, etc.). This allows you to talk to your ba anytime, in the car, on the bus, on the way to work, while running, at the park, on the beach, in the woods, wherever.

Since everyone has a *ba* and our *ba* knows everything about us, and all the good that occurs to us is because of our *ba*. If there is something in our life that we do not like it is because we have not expressed it to our *ba*. Here I must offer a word of caution, which is not to complain too much about something you dislike in your life that you asked for. This is because our *ba* similar to our *sahu* does not distinguish when we are just venting or are seriously dissatisfied with an aspect of our life. Its job is to connect us with the Divine and help us to achieve our destiny.

Using my experience as an example, I asked for a "spiritual woman" because I thought that with a "spiritual woman" it would be a lot easier to live with this individual. I expected that a woman interested in the same spiritual discipline as I, would be willing to do meditation rituals with me, so that we could spiritually evolve and be able to figuratively "conquer the world." That of course was not the case. Instead I found myself using every bit of spiritual strength I could muster to keep from doing something totally out of character. The fact that this individual was interested in spiritual matters only complicated issues even more. For a while I was angry at my *ba* but it was not my *ba's* fault. It was only doing what I (my *ab*) told it to do and helping me to fulfill my destiny. Once I realized this that is when I learned my lesson and never made the same mistake.

But, another point I want to make about this example is that the reason my *ba* brought this situation to me was because of my erroneous beliefs. It was what I thought a "spiritual woman" was based upon past experiences. Past experiences or past memories remember are governed by our *sahu*. It is our *sahu* that makes us think that the grass on the other side is greener or that ice from another icemaker is colder. This is why now, when I ask my *ba* for something, I leave my options open and let it decide what is best for me, since it knows more than my *sahu*.

Chapter 4:
The Kamitic Theology

Years before Kamit became a powerful empire and an institution of learning in ancient times. According to the "Out of Africa" theory that is widespread amongst anthropologists these days. The first human beings emerged in Africa, but some of these early human beings or ancient Africans according to the geographical history migrated to the Northeastern part of Asia. While another group migrated to Europe and the Northwestern part of Asia, but a substantial number of these ancient people stayed in the continent of Africa and migrated to the southern part of Europe and Western and Central Asia. But life for these early human beings was not as we know it today.

Human beings in ancient times lived in the most horrid and harshest way because the Maa had not established itself in our world. As a result, ravenous beasts and climatic changes preyed upon early man and woman. They were constantly in search of food and shelter, until some of these nomadic people in Africa discovered the north flowing, Nile River, which provided some peace of mind. Due to the annual inundation of the Nile, which made the soil – particularly the southern region – fertile, thus attracting wild game, the Nile seemed to be a physical manifestation of *nyun*. The great river seemed to be an endless source of food for the ancient man and woman, so eventually these nomadic people began to settle alongside the riverbanks. Then they organize themselves into tribes and later tribal clans in relation to the Nile. The tribal clans that had settled near the south of the Nile called this southern region KM-T commonly translated as Kamit or KAM–Ta, which means "the Black Lands." The term initially was a reference to the dark fertile that was produced due to the inundation of the Nile, but it soon would take on a different meaning. The tribal clans that settled along the north of the Nile called this region T-ST or Ta–SETT, which means "the Red Lands." This was because the region unlike its southern neighbor was dry and arid as the Nile snaked its way towards the Mediterranean Sea.

These tribal clans of the south and north, who depended upon the Nile for their survival, ironically became autonomous and rivals of each other because of the Great River. Eventually this rivalry erupted into a great civil war allegorized as the *Story of Osar*.

The Story of Osar

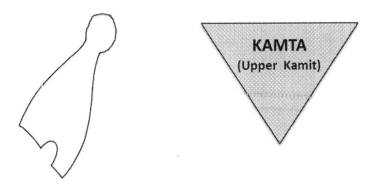

Hedjet[7]: White Crown of Kamit & KAMTA (The Black Lands)

According to some versions of the story, there were five children known as the Children of Rau (also called the Children of Nut and Geb in some versions). They were Osar, Oset, Hruur (Hruaakahuti), Nebhet and Set. At the time, Ra was the ruler of both lands but had become so old and feeble (Ra Atum) that he decided to relinquish his throne to his successors. It is said in some versions that Ra initially passed the reign to Osar but in other versions. It is claimed that Ra split his kingdom amongst the two lands and passed sovereignty of the southern region KAMTA to Osar, who became the owner of the white Hedjet crown. While the northern region, TASETT passed to Set, who became the owner of the red Deshret crown.

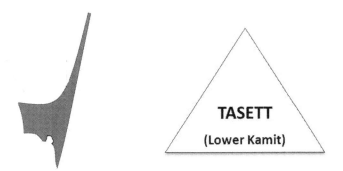

Deshret: The Red Crown of Kamit & TASETT (The Red Lands)

---

[7] It should be noted that the root of the word "Hedjet" is the word "djet" which means "backbone" a reference to "inner strength."

At the time, both lands were ravaged by civil strife and Osar desiring to bring peace to his war torn kingdom searched for ways to unite the people. Upon doing so he discovered the Maa and taught it to his people. Then he taught them the science of agriculture, which laid the foundation for the society to become a prosperous kingdom. In a relatively short time the teachings of Osar spread throughout the land like wildfire. Men no longer fought with each other over trivial matters. Instead they worked together for a common objective.

Everyone loved and was eternally grateful to Osar for what he had done, except for Set who had become insanely jealous of Osar's fame and success. So much so that he plotted with several conspirators to kill Osar. Unbeknownst to the great king, Set had a great celebration for his oldest brother. When Osar was drunk and full from ale, Set and his conspirators murdered him. Later Set hacked up Osar's body into 14 pieces[8] and scattered it throughout the land. Immediately following Osar's death Set usurped the throne and ruled the land with his wife Nebhet (Nephtys).

All was lost as the great kingdom fell into disarray because no one would dare challenge Set. Thankfully, Oset, Osar's loving and devoted wife, despite the bounty upon her head, managed to magically conceive an heir for Osar, whom she named Hru (Horus). Then, she secretly recovered all of the pieces of Osar's body with the help of her guide Npu (Anubis in Greek) and Nebhet, who left Set after all of his misdeeds.

When Hru had come of age, he received a dream from Osar telling him to avenge his father's wrongful death. In some versions it is said that Hruaakhuti (also known as Hru Ur – Hru the Elder) tried to defeat Set but was unable to do so, because Set was too powerful. This is an allusion to the fact that you can't fight fire with fire.

So, the young prince Hru raised an army and challenged Set for the throne. After several battles were fought, Hru found that he was unable to defeat his older and more military experienced uncle on the battlefield. Then, on one decisive battle, Set had managed to get close enough to Hru to actually gouge out the young prince's eye. Fleeing for his life, Hru retreated to the safety of his father's trusted vizier Djahuti (Thoth), who was able to repair Hru's eye perfectly.

---

[8] The hacking of the body of Osar symbolizes soul loss or the fragmentation of the soul.

When Hru returned back to the battlefield, he could see Set's weaknesses perfectly and when he got close enough to his uncle. He cut the seat of his pants out (some version says he castrated Set). Then he dragged the defeated ruler to be judged by Oset. But the wife Osar refused to condemn Set to death on the ground that that despite his evil doings. He was still Osar's brother, so she freed Set from his bonds and allowed him to go free. Angered by his mother's sympathy and her decision to free Set, Hru in a fit of rage with his sword cut Ouut's head off (in some versions he cut off her diadem), which was magically restored by Djahuti to remind him that he was the king, meaning Set was his responsibility and not his mother's.

After Set was freed it wasn't long after that he began rousing up ruckus again. Since, no one would remove him from power because his sway was too strong. He began a viscous campaign proclaiming that Hru was not the legitimate heir of Osar, and therefore not fit to rule the land. The campaign was so successful that the matter was finally taken before a tribunal to decide who would rule the kingdom. Just like the battle on the battlefield. The tribunal could not decide who should rule. Some argued for Set and his power of might, while others sided with Hru and declared that he was by all means the legitimate ruler. Then, Djahuti suggested that the spirit of Osar as Tum be allowed to speak on Hru's behalf.

Osar spoke and reminded the tribunal of all of the things he had done to build the kingdom they were in. He reminded them of the Maa and how he introduced to them the science of agriculture. He then issued a warning telling the tribunal that if they did not do what is right, justice would find a way to be served.

Upon hearing Osar's plea, the tribunal found Hru to be true of voice and found Set guilty of breaking the very laws he swore to uphold. As a result, Set was punished to spread the teachings of Osar, by telling of his misdeeds and explaining how Hru and Osar defeated him. Hru, who was robbed of his heritage, had his name and legacy viciously soiled by Set, through Osar's words and the tribunal's decision was purified of all accusations and made whole again. The heir of Osar was later awarded both the upper and lower crowns of the kingdom. Thereby, declaring that a righteous leader and individual is like Hru who is reserve in speech, has self – control (controls over his or her passions) and thinks before he or she acts, instead of allowing their emotions to betray them while harming themselves and others.

54

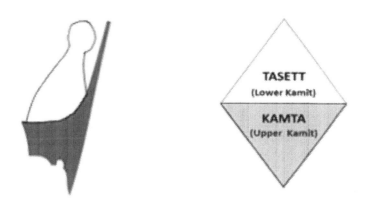

Pschent: Double Crown of Kamit & United Kingdom

The unification of the country restored the Maa – the Balance, Law, Justice, and Righteousness – throughout the land. Hru as a result, became the perfect example of what a true leader, ruler and child of God are supposed to be like, which is an individual that is not overly aggressive or too passive. But, level headed and well balanced, because are in the world but not of the world.

The term TASETT came to represent the outer regions of the country in a multidimensional manner. Anything and everything that was seen as being a hostile was identified as being TASETT and associated with the physical world. KAMTA on the other hand was associated with everything that was spiritual and required contemplation such as the ancestors, stars, cemeteries, tombs, night sky, mystery systems, etc. KAMTA or Kamit was eventually adopted by the people as the name of their country, as a physical reminder of the dark color of the soil, but chiefly to claim allegiance and identify themselves with their spiritual patriarch Osar. For this reason, when referring to the realm on the maa aankh, KAMTA[9] is capitalized but when speaking of the system we use the word Kamta.

---

[9] There are many terms used to represent the underworld, such as Aaru, Amenta, and Tuat. Due to dogma and misunderstanding of the Kamitic concepts and principles, which has led many to interpret the underworld to be a literal eternal resting place such as heaven or hell? KAMTA is being used in its place to remind the reader that the spiritual realm is the polar opposite of the physical realm.

The Basis of Kamitic Spirituality

Now, no one really knows if the *Story of Osar* was an actual historical event or not, because it is ancient story older than all of the religious books combined. As a result, the story has become a mythical legend that takes on a new meaning each time it is told to a new generation. What is known however is that according to Kamitic history around the 32nd century BCE. The first ruler of Kamit was a man named Narmer also known as Menes, who is commonly shown defeating his enemies on a palette while wearing the white Hedjet crown (the same white crown of Osar). Narmer or Menes' successor was a man named Aha or Hru-Aha, who was the second ruler in the first dynasty in Kamit, which means that the story (like most great stories) was probably inspired by true events. King Narmer and King Hru Aha were either biologically and/or spiritually related. This means according to the *Story of Osar* the basis of Kamitic spirituality focused on self – development by working with one's ancestral spirits. This implies that Osar was Hru's spirit guide, which was the basis of Kamitic spirituality and later Christianity.

What about Jesus and Kamitic Spirituality?

Working with one's guardian spirit and spirit guides, was the original purpose of Christianity. It is well known that because Kamit was the most advance, economically secured and influential civilization that existed during ancient times. Early writers of the major contemporary religions borrowed many of their concepts in the development of their religion, but the religion that borrowed the most was Christianity. There have been numerous Christian artifacts found in Egypt tying the Kamitic and early Christian tradition together, so much so that Sir E.A. Wallis Budge after comparing the Kamitic tradition and the Christianity noted that

> *The new religion (Christianity) which was preached there by St. Mark and his immediate followers, in all essentials so closely resembled that which was the outcome of the worship of Osiris, Isis, and Horus that popular opposition was entirely disarmed.*

Christianity practiced today is distinctly different from the Kamitic tradition because the characters in the Kamitic tradition are metaphors, whereas the characters in the Christian version are said to be actual people. For instance, whereas Narmer is associated with Osar and every other king following him is associated with Hru, thus creating a sustaining tradition. In Christianity Osar becomes the Great Jehovah or the Great Christian God, and Jesus of Nazareth is quickly identified with Hru, so there is no other divinely inspired individual that exists according to Christian lore. Everything in regards to Hru from his immaculate birth, to the visitation from the three wise kings and attempt on the young child's life, and even his mythical ascension is interpreted as being a literal event that occurred to Jesus in Christianity.

Now that more Christian artifacts have been recovered (the *Books of Thomas, the Gospel of Mary, the Protovangelion of James, the Gospel of Nicodemus,* etc.) we see that not all early Christians thought and believed the same way. There were several sects of Christianity that existed throughout the region and most of the early Christians were Jewish people. The Christian sect that suppressed the others, which also deified Jesus of Nazareth from a man and made him God incarnate, was the Roman Catholic Christian sect. This came about because after the Roman Emperor Constantine converted to Christianity. In an effort to expand and manage his empire, Constantine created the Council of Nicaea in 325 A.D. to centralize the core Christian beliefs. It was at this council the dogma of Jesus was created and Jesus Christ became synonymous with God.

Jesus however never equated himself with the Supreme Being. In fact, when you read what Jesus says to his disciples. He speaks like an ambassador, diplomat, messenger or representative sent by a higher authority. Most of the time when Jesus speaks he refers to God as his Father or the One who sent him. Consider the following passages:

"Whoever acknowledges me before men, I will also acknowledge him before my Father in heaven. But whoever disowns me before men, I will disown him before my Father in heaven." (Mathew 10:32)

At that time, Jesus said in reply, *"I give praise to you Father, Lord of heaven and earth, for although you have hidden these things from the wise and the learned you have revealed them to the childlike. Yes, Father, such has been your gracious will. All things have been handed over to me by my Father, and no one knows the Father except the son and anyone to whom the son wishes to reveal him."* (Matthew 11: 25-27)

"Whoever receives one child such as this in my name, receives me; and whoever receives me, receives not me but the One who sent me." (Mark 9:36-37)

"But I have testimony greater than John's. But the works that the Father gave me to accomplish, these works that I perform testify on my behalf that the Father has sent me. Moreover, the Father who sent me has testified on my behalf." (John 6: 36-37)

And said to them, *"Whoever welcomes this little child in my name welcomes me; and whoever welcomes me welcomes the one who sent me. For the one who is least among you all-he is the greatest."* (Luke 9:48)

So Jesus cried out in the temple area as he was teaching and said, *"You know me and also know where I am from. Yet I did not come on my own, but the one who sent me, whom you do not know, is true. I know him, because I am from Him and He sent me."* (John 7: 28-29)

If Jesus were God, when the disciples asked how do we talk to the Father he would have said you just pray to me, but he didn't. He instead taught them to pray by beginning with the phrase, "Our Father."

When it is accepted that Jesus is not God incarnate but was an ordinary man. Who according to biblical accounts, with his parents fled to Egypt and returned to Nazareth before the age of 12, which meant he spent around ten years in Egypt and had some knowledge of Kamitic lore. Then when we review the accounts and read that when Jesus became an adult, he was baptized, began preaching and transcended his ego. Jesus becomes the perfect role model revealing that the way to connect God is by following your spirit(s). This explains the reason Jesus says, *"God is spirit, and his worshipers must worship in spirit and truth"* *(John 4:34).*

The spirit that Jesus is speaking of is your higher spirit and your higher spirits. Jesus was teaching his followers who believed in God but didn't know God for themselves, because Jewish tradition had made God out to be an unapproachable and vengeful Deity. By using himself as an example, Jesus was able to speak to God directly because of his righteous living and told those who felt that they could not speak directly to God. That they could talk to God through the assistance of their higher spirits, who are believed to reside with the Divine. This new form of spirituality that Jesus was teaching was considered radical because it was remotely similar to communing with the dead, which Jewish law forbade. Jesus however assured his followers that it was not the same but that he was following the Spirit. This is the reason Roman Catholicism being the eldest and most established of the Christian sects continues to this day to honor and venerate Christian martyrs and saints.

58

This new spirituality that Jesus was teaching was inspired by the Kamitic tradition because it was the true philosophy behind venerating the ancestors. Kamitic spirituality contrary to archeological belief was not spiritualism – the belief and practice that we can communicate with the dead. Kamitic spirituality focused on working with the higher spirits so that one could do the things that Jesus did in his life. Hru was used as a metaphor symbolizing the transcending of one's ego to better serve God and the people.

We see from Jesus' life that spiritual development is not accomplished by sitting in a room intellectualizing or contemplating the nature of the universe. It is accomplished by living your life according to the principles of Maa.

Maa: The Absolute Truth

The Maa (pronounced Ma'au or Ma'aw also called Maat) was the philosophic concept that guided Kamitic way of life and believed by some to be the origin of African philosophy.   But, if you ask anyone that has seriously studied the Kamitic history and their spiritual texts what is the Maa. You most likely will get a different interpretation from each because the Maa is a very difficult concept to accurately explain in Western terms. The reason it is difficult for most people in the West to understand the Maa is because, Westerners are accustomed to being corralled by religious authorities and told what to do and what not to do. Even though many Westerners may disagree with a religious concept for whatever reason, out of fear, the pious are discouraged from questioning any concept because to do so is believed that they are questioning God (or the man of God) and will go to hell. On the other hand, if the pious simply accepts and follows what they are told, it is believed they will ascend to heaven. This is the same threat and reward tactic that is used to govern most of Western society, which is why it is difficult for most Westerners to imagine a society without the same type of restrictive guidelines. But, Kamit (and many other African societies inspired and/or influenced by the Kamitic tradition) did function without this threat and reward method that parents use on their children, and authority figures use on the masses of society, in order to get people to act ethically and morally.

In Kamitic spirituality people didn't believe that God rewards an individual for their good deeds by calling them to heaven and punishing the wicked by sending them to hell. This was because in part they didn't believe in an ethereal realm called heaven or a fiery place in the middle of the earth called hell. What they believed in was that there was a spiritual realm that consisted of different spiritual levels ranging from low to high. In order for an individual to ascend to the higher levels they had to have demonstrated that they had the self – discipline and self – mastery to be there, sort of like ascending to a higher grade in grade school. For instance, if an individual is hindered by a strong negative emotion such as fear, guilt, worry, etc. or is addicted to some substance (alcohol, drugs, etc.). Then just like this individual in plagued by these inhibitions in life they will continue to be plagued by them in death and would pass to a lower level in the spiritual realm, which was very close to the physical realm. However, if an individual in life was ethical, moral, self-discipline, reserved in speech, etc., then this individual would ascend to the higher levels in the spiritual realm, which was closer to the Divine. The reason is because Maa meant "balance", "law", "order", "reciprocity", "righteousness", and "truth", but it also loosely meant "the Way", "Holistic Living/Thinking", "The Right Way", "The Path" and "True Love." Everything that existed in the universe was a reflection of something else. This meant that death according to the Maa was just a mirror reflection of an individual's life. So whatever an individual did in life is what that individual would continue to do in death. We therefore, make our own heaven and hell.

Thus, the Maa was somewhat like the Hindu concept of karma and the Chinese Tao, with a slight difference being that people did not obsess over past incarnations (or karmic debt) as they do today. Nor did they threaten people with the idea that if they didn't live right or worship God that they were going to go to hell. Instead one was encouraged to live each day in the present with death in mind. This may seem a little morbid to the Western mind, but the theory was that if one always kept death in mind. Such as what you would like people to remember about you or the understanding that one day you would have to stand before your ancestors and explain to them your wrong doings. This type of thinking made people more conscientious about their actions and behavior and forced them to see that their death would be a reflection of their life. If they treat people with love, honor and respect. They will receive the same just treatment upon their death, which would relieve them of the greatest pain there was, the heavy burden of guilt.

Chapter 5:
The Kamitic Spiritual Universe

The purpose of life therefore is to strive to become an enlightened ancestor. This is how Jesus became the greatest Christian ancestor followed by Saint Peter, which is why the tomb (or bones) of Peter is under St. Peter's Basilica. This has always been about the survival of life after death and how spirits come into existence.

There are numerous theories as to how and why spirits exist. The most accepted and scientific theory is that developed by French educator Hippolyte Léon Denizard Rivail (1804 – 1869 better known by his pen name Allan Kardec).

The Spiritual Universe According to Kardecism

Kardec, the astronomy, chemistry, mathematics and physics teacher, was a meticulous investigator. By relying upon mediums and thoroughly investigating their response. He discovered through spirit communication that God is the Supreme Intelligence, the Original Cause of Everything, the Creator of the Universe and All within it. Spirits therefore are intelligent beings Created by God and the community of all the spirits connected is what is commonly referred to as the Spirit or Holy Spirit. Human beings are therefore incarnated spirits composed of a body soul (spirit), which means everything is essentially a spirit. Since our universe is composed of a physical and spiritual world, Kardec learned that the Law of Cause and Effect governed the universe. This means for every action there is a reaction; our actions (positive or negative) will have a similar effect on our present life, afterlife or reincarnation.

Based upon his research, Kardec learned that spirits evolve intellectually and morally by setting their own path toward spiritual perfection. Spiritual progress occurs from having human experiences, which allows us to learn compassion, forgiveness and love. Since likes attracts likes. Spiritual communication between human beings occurs because a like mind attracts spirits of a similar vibration. Therefore, there are three types of spirits that exist and they are:

1. First Order – Pure Spirits
2. Second Order – Good Spirits (High, Wise, Learned and Benevolent Spirits).
3. Third Order – Imperfect Spirits (Boisterous, Neutral, Trickster, Frivolous and Impure Spirits)

Kardec's theory of the universe according to my experience and research seems to coincide exactly with the Kamitic belief of the spiritual universe.

Tarrying for the Spirit

Most people believe that the Holy Spirit is a Ghost or Divine Spirit, but in truth it is the life force or cosmic energy that exists in all things (animated and inanimate). When a person dies, their *ab* soul continues to exist because it is the immortal part of the human being and they become a spirit. The spirit merges with the Rau where it continues to exist in the spiritual – KAMTA plane. When a living individual holds a particular thought in his or her mind for a long period of time, the thoughts of the individual is what attracts the type of spirits to them.

For instance, I remember before salvation became big business how there used to be a Prayer Room and this is how people in the olden days use to get the Holy Ghost. The Prayer Room was funky. I mean it smelled funky and had that funky vibe like people had been throwing down (in a good way). There would be a woman or several women called missionaries (usually dressed in white and red, reminding me of the Santeria *Francisca*) that would go to this room with you with a bunch of other people. In this little cramped up, no ventilation room (because it was always hot) there would be pews surrounding the walls. Sometimes in one corner there would be a stack of old beat up bibles with curled covers. You would go kneel on the floor and repeat only two phrases, "Thank you Jesus" and "Hallelujah" over and over. Eventually, you would do it so much that you would begin speaking gibberish or what is called "speaking in tongues," because none of what you said makes logical sense. This is how you knew you got the Holy Ghost. This is what was called *Tarrying for the Spirit.*

Now, the fact that I grew up in the church and saw people get struck by the Spirit who would speak in tongues in a minute, then right after they left church would revert right back to their backstabbing, lying, cheating and you name it, hellish ways. I had to conclude that these people weren't struck by the "Holy Spirit" but simply by a "spirit", and that spirit most likely was someone that was very close to them. Of course, if this individual had been properly educated about spirits they would have known that their actions, behaviors and thoughts attracted certain types of spirits to them. This is the reason most likely the individual reverted back to their old ways.

Three Types of Spirits

The above experience made me concur with Kardec that there are three classes of spirits but I have found their arrangement to be slightly different. Since spirits were once human beings that do not have a physical body, which gives them the ability to go anywhere at any time instantly; and spirits mainly influence our thought, which influences our actions and behaviors. This means that the types of spirits that exist are determined by their conscious development or spiritual maturity. There are therefore highly evolved spirits, averaged developed spirits and lowly spirits, with the latter having the spiritual maturity similar to an animal or beast. In other words, when it is compared with the cosmology of the soul (See Chapter 3), there are spirits that have perfected their *ab*. Then there are spirits that are in the process of developing their *ab*. And, lastly there are spirits whose *ab* is underdeveloped.

Keeping in mind that the *ab* corresponds to our ability to concentrate and focus our will. It can be said that the spirits that have perfected their *ab* basically mastered the ability to influence the physical world, because they are self-disciplined. Whereas those with an underdeveloped *ab* have allowed the influences of the physical world to master their *ab*, resulting in them being undisciplined. It is like these lower spirits basically have scattered thoughts and do not have the ability to concentrate on their own, which is why these ghostly entities must leech on to someone to save them and show them the right way.

This is why so much emphasis was placed upon developing the *ab*, but the Kamitic people didn't believe in taking a class on meditation to improve and strengthen the *ab*. They created a cultural way of life to cultivate the *ab* of its citizens. It was based upon the understanding that many of these spirits carrying elemental traits associated with places in nature such as the streets, the mountains, the forests, the ocean, lakes, etc.

are all places where these spirits reside. These spirits when linked to the maa aankh (See below) are called:

1. Netcharu are archetypical guides or guardian angels.
2. Aakhu are ancestral spirits and spirit guides.
3. Aapepu are misguided, malevolent, earthbound trickster spirits[10].

As a result, higher spirits appeal to our *ba*, while lower spirits appeal to our *sahu* because they are closer to the living, but it is with our *ab* we have to decide which to listen to. To cultivate the *ab*, the Kamitic culture focused on helping one to learn how to interact with these non-physical forces that exist in our universe.

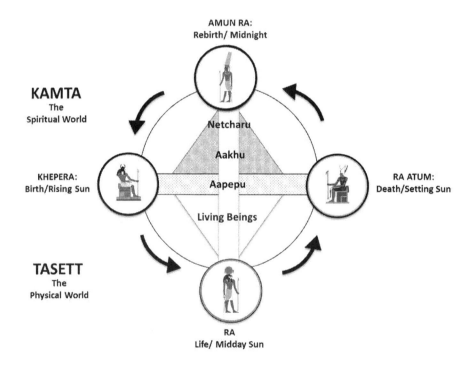

The Spiritual Universe According to the Maa Aankh
(Please note that the maa aankh is upside down)

---

[10] The maa aankh represents the physical and spiritual realm below. The lower the spirit the closer the spirit is to the physical realm or TASETT.

64

Netcharu: Archetypical Guardian Spirits

The Netcharu are deified ancestral spirits that have become linked with nature and act as archetypes or guardian spirits for all of humanity. They are emissaries for the Divine and can appear to anyone regardless of their beliefs. For instance, when the Africans were brought to North America, the loss of African theology caused these spirits to syncretize with the Protestant biblical tradition. One of the most popular spirits from this religious syncretism is Moses, an associate of Npu that inspired Harriet Tubman and the Underground Railroad. But, they have other identifications such as to the various angels in the *Book of Enoch* and other attributes of God. There are nine major netcharu and these spirits are seen as spiritual tribal clan leaders from the *Story of Osar*. The nine netcharu are:

1. **Osar** – is the netchar of knowledge, wisdom, purity and rebirth. He is Lord of all of the netcharu and is seen as mystic light. Osar is associated with Jesus because he represents the orderly use of power and an enlightened consciousness due to rebirth. Osar is the foundation of everything. He lies underground, therefore avalanches and earthquakes are seen as attempts made by Set to usurp him. Osar is fond of all things white such as milk, coconut milk, rice, boiled yucca, potatoes, etc., but never offer him alcoholic beverages. All days are sacred to him but he is fond of Sunday.

2. **Oset** is the devoted wife of Osar and therefore queen mother of the people. She represents the feminine principle of creation. She represents our instinctive desire to survive emotionally, mentally, spiritually and physically. She is generally linked to the sea, the crescent moon and is associated with Virgin Mary. Her colors are bright blue or turquoise. Her sacred day is Monday (Mood-day). Her sacred number is seven. She is fond of melons, seashells, fish, fishing nets, molasses, beer, pineapples and rum.

3. **Npu** is the netchar of the roads, the divine messenger and the divine guide. He is incorrectly linked to the devil because he like Hru stands in the middle of the maa aankh due to his cunningness. He is associated with Joseph the Dreamer and Moses. Npu's colors are red, black and white, and sometimes

yellow which links him to the Maa. Npu is fond of rum, cigars, candy, fruits, sweet treats, corn, and popcorn.

4. **Hru** is the true heir to the throne of Osar and the lord of justice. He represents the manliness of men, authoritative power and the lightning bolt. He is associated with the biblical King David. His colors are red and white. He is called upon when someone wants justice. His sacred number is six. He is fond of apples, rum, beer and spicy foods. His special day is Sunday.

5. **Djahuti** – is the netchar of divination and is associated with the biblical King Solomon. His colors are royal blue and white. He accepts the same gifts as Osar.

6. **Nebhet** is netchar love, money, sensuality and rivers. She is associated with the biblical Ruth and Mary Magdalene. She represents beauty, immature and youthful feminine passion. Her colors are yellow, pink, yellow and green. Her sacred number is five and her special day is Friday. She is fond of passion fruits, honey, spinach, shrimp, oranges, rum, light beers, cantaloupe and pumpkins.

7. **Hruaakhuti** is the warrior netchar that governs and protects soldiers in the military. He is associated with the apostle Peter. He represents hard work, our ability to act quickly and defend ourselves within certain parameters. Hruaakhuti's colors are blood red and sometimes purple. He is called upon when one needs to fight. His special day is Tuesday the day of Mars and his numbers are 3, 4, 7 and 11. He is fond of hearty and rustic foods like roasted root vegetables, wild game and anything that hunters like. He enjoys strong cigars, rum, vodka and whiskey.

8. **Maat** is sometimes said to be the sister of Djahuti or the wife of Hruaakhuti, whatever the case she is the protector of the Maa and thereby the protector of Nature. She is associated with John the Baptist the last protector of the Old Testament. Her colors are sky blue, light blue and yellow. She works closely with the Native American aakhu. Her

special number is 2 and 4. Her special day is Thursday. She is rustic foods but enjoys fruits, nuts, corn, rum and water.

9. **Sokar** is the Lord of the Cemetery and Disease. He is associated with the biblical Job and the parable Lazarus. I have also found him to be identified with Saint Alex (Alexis or San Alejo). His colors are indigo and black but because of his prowess he is honored with white, brown or purples. He is called upon whenever one wants assistance in healing. He is fond of rum, cigars, dry white wines, sesame seeds, grains, legumes, dates and raisins. His sacred day is Saturday. His special numbers are 13 and 17.

Please note that the above guidelines are based upon my personal observations.

Aakhu: Ancestral Spirits & Spirit Guides

Aakhu are ancestral spirits commonly referred to as guardian angels, guiding spirits or benevolent spirits. Majority of the aakhu are usually one's deceased elderly relative that appear in our dreams as Osar had done with Hru, but a lot of the aakhu are benevolent unrelated spirits that take an interest in our affairs and just want to see us succeed. These spirits are what Kardec referred to as Good Spirits can be the spirits of Native Americans, Asians or from some other nationality. For instance, an astute martial arts student may attract the attention of his master's deceased teacher, which is why many martial artists pay homage to the founder of their school. Most aakhu are associated or work under the guidance of a netcharu rather they know it or not. For instance, Native American aakhu are fond of working with Maat and so on.

Aapepu: Confused, Misguided, Earthbound Spirits

Aapepu is the general term used to describe the lowest types of spirits that exist[11]. They are very close to the TASETT because majority of them are

---

[11] These negative spirits were called Sebau, which were individuals in life that caused a great amount of evil due to following the wrong beliefs and

earthbound entities. Originally they were the negative spirits that were outcast from the Kamitic society that were commonly called the enemies of Rau. But, they are the incestuous parents, the sadistic aunts and uncles, the murdering, drug peddling, stealing and thieving individuals that we want out of our life and never want to hear from again. Keeping in mind that it is the choices that we make that determine our fate in the afterlife and that those who do not follow their *ba*. Live their life and therefore their death in misery. Most aapepu aren't evil as filmmakers portray them, although some are e.g. Hitler). Majority of these spirits are confused and misguided ghosts because in life they were confused and misguided people who blamed everyone else for the problems they had in life. As a result of their poor decision-making, most aapepu when alive died in a horrible, shameful and/or violent manner – usually by accident, homicide or suicide. Just like in life these negative people were avoided because of their failure to change their conscious ways, resulting in them attracting all sorts of dangers to them. In death they are avoided (and rarely mentioned) as well because they can easily sway the living into making the same unwise decisions they made in life. In Kamit these spirits were regarded as being noxious worms or serpents that resided in the wilderness. In other parts of Africa like in the Kongo, they were seen as noxious lizards roaming gravesites. When the Africans were brought to North America, these spirits adapted to the new environment and were anthropomorphized as the "blues" in the African American blues music tradition and the devils. In contemporary times the aapepu are seen as roaming the alleys and street corners of the cities. A lot of times aapepu sit outside beneath the front doorstep, this is the reason why it is customary in African and many Asian traditions to erect shrines and paint them red at entryways to deter these hungry ghosts[12] from entering ones dwelling.

You can tell when an aapepu is near because they give off a vibe of confusion, ignorance, laziness, misguidance, stubbornness, sluggishness, depressive, etc. They are the invisible forces that tempt us to take the easy and unethical way to achieve our dreams, which is why they are so closely associated with Set. This is why most aapepu are avoided because they have the uncanny ability to encourage people to feed their

---

ideas, like most tyrants. They were also called Nak, which refers to a lack of spiritual light or spiritual ignorance.

[12] Red is the color of fire, defense, warning, etc. It is used to frighten negative energies.

destructive habits like addiction to alcohol or drugs, or engage in low emotional states like anger, anxiety, fear, guilt, rage, revenge, sadness, etc. Thereby preventing people from evolving in life, one of the easiest ways to keep them at bay is by creating a thought form by repeating a prayer, like the Lord's Prayer, which is excellent for assisting one in keeping a positive mindset that repels negative spirits.

Set it should be clearly understood was not and is not evil incarnate. To make such an assumption would cause one to fall for the greatest trick ever, which is to look for a physical impish devilish creature while totally missing that Set is a spiritual energy that can manifest itself in anyone. Set was the original ruler of TASETT because he represents youthful, masculine, passionate and curious energy, which all youth possess. What makes him evil is the direction and path that this energy takes to manifests him. This is why he is associated with Cain, Judas Iscariot and the devil. He is considered to be the first outcast and therefore the first of the aapepu, because his energy is raw, unadulterated, and uncontrollable. Everything he does, like a bully, is by physical force[13]. He rules by fear, which is why to oppose him one needs to have courage and the ability to connect with those on the other side, spiritual world. The physical manifestation of Set is war, wild fire, storms, hurricanes, etc.

Something you have to understand about spirits is that just like there are no two people that are exactly the same, spirits are not exactly alike either. The only way logically for one spirit to be everywhere at the same time is by having delegates or representatives. If you think of KAMTA as being a mirror reflection of TASETT you will see that just there are good people, there are good spirits. Just like there are bad people, there are also bad spirits, which means that everyone has netcharu, aakhu and aapepu. Each of these spirits is unique in their own way because we are unique in our own way. The descriptions given above are therefore general information about these spirits; so don't expect your spirit to be exactly as described above. This is why all information from spirits should be scrutinized to the utmost degree. By doing this I have found that generally speaking since higher spirits lived this life and are aware of trials and tribulations. They tend to be more patient and forgiving, while lower spirits tend to be more impatient.

---

[13] This is also the reason why he is so closely associated with Ra because this moment refers to when our *ab* is at its highest physically.

69

To attract the benevolent influences of your netcharu and aakhu, while keeping the aapepu at bay, you have to learn how to a bit of mind control. This is because as you remember, spirits influence our thoughts so if you don't think evil. You will not attract evil influences to you and so on. So, one of the easiest ways to develop mind control is by creating sacred space. When you create sacred space you make an elusive concept and principle concrete, so that when there is blockage or a problem in an individual's life. The sacred space can be referred to in order to acquire clarity on how to implement constructive change.

Creating Sacred Space

Sacred space or an altar is a meeting place where you and your spirits come together to discuss issues. It can be as simple as drawing an X on the ground or as complex as the altars used in the Catholic Church. The reason altars are used in this practice is because besides being a great way to honor your netcharu and aakhu. They help you to learn how to develop your *ba* intuition, because it is a go as you feel type of practice. You are in total control of this entire process. You are not by any means obligated to do anything. If you at any time feel that something is not right you can remove it. Or, if you feel that something is needed you can add it because there are not a lot of rules you have to follow. The main purpose of this practice is to help you to develop your intuition by overcoming your fears of working with spirits.

The altars used in this practice are commonly called *bovedas* or spiritual altars, which have been adapted from the Afro – Cuban Cruzado Espiritismo tradition. I personally prefer to call these spiritual houses because through my experience this is what they have become, dwellings for the spirits. As a result, they have come to look more and more like homes, which is why I prefer to call them *het*, Kamitic for house.

Now, there are many ways these spiritual houses or hets[14] can be constructed. In this regard, you are only limited by your imagination and space. Since the point however is not to just make an aesthetic space but a functional sacred space that will allow for spiritual communication through meditation and prayer. You are free to make your hets as creatively as you want, but you must follow the **Spiritual Hierarchy**

---

[14] Technically "u" is used to pluralize Kamitic words.

according to the maa aankh as explained above. This is because the hets tend to take on a type of *feng shui* approach in its construction and erection, which you will soon see. That being said, you are free to set up your hets in any direction dictated first by space availability. If you have adequate space, you may want to set up your spiritual house in the southern direction, so that when you stand (or sit) in front of it you are facing the south. This is not necessary but makes it easier for you to correspond to the rising and setting of the sun in relation to the maa aankh.

Het Aakhu – Ancestral Spiritual House

There are two types of hets that can be constructed. All of the other individual hets are just modifications of these two. The most important of these hets is the spiritual house for your aakhu or *het aakhu*. If you can only build one het because of limited space then this is the altar to build. To construct the het aakhu you will need the following:

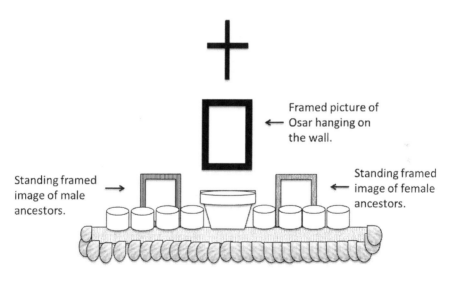

Simple Kamta Het (Spiritual House/Altar)

- A bare crucifix (with no image on it) or the Eye of Ra to symbolize Amun Ra.

71

- A small table, box, bookshelf or any flat surface that has been cleaned of debris and covered with a white cloth (optional).

- Photos of your aakhu placed in silver or gold colored picture frames (which indicate that these spirits have ascended to a higher plane of existence). The photos should only have images of those who have made transition. Never put photos of living people on the altar. You can also have dolls or icons symbolizing your aakhu. Also do not hang your aakhu on the walls. This is reserved for the netcharu. Male ancestors are placed on your left and female ancestors are placed on the right. It is also customary to put a figurine of an old African man and woman to symbolize the first ancestors brought to the Americas, whose wisdom survives even in this tradition[15].

- A large clear goblet and eight glasses of water (which symbolizes the nine netcharu, the nine directions and nine major spiritual forces that exist in the universe. The water is used to clarify the channels for spiritual communication to easily take place and provide spiritual nourishment. The water in the glasses should be kept full throughout the week and replaced at least once a week. The large is always placed in the middle, with four placed to the left (symbolizing the masculine aspect of nature) and four to the right (symbolizing the feminine aspect of nature).

- White seashells[16] are used to form a border (symbolizing the spiritual realm). For extra potency the seashells can be covered with cascarilla, efun or white pemba (consecrated chalks that can be purchased at most Latin American spiritual supply stores) or regular chalk if none is available.

- White candles the size of birthday candles and cigars.

---

[15] Kamitic spirituality is always about balance. Maa is always in the picture balancing energies and forces.

[16] In most Afro-Latino traditions chalk was used to mark off sacred space, but African Americans lacking the available African resources used instead naturally white or painted white seashells. The color white is the color of the white Hedjet crown symbol of knowledge, wisdom, purity and strength.

72

- A small jar or cup to be filled with Florida Water and other personal colognes or perfumes.

- A glass ashtray should be filled with sand to hold incense and cigars.

- A candleholder.

- A bible (New Living Translation Bible if you are new to reading it) or Book of Psalms and Proverbs. Remember our intention is for spiritual practice and since most of our spirits were Christian or familiar with this faith. The bible becomes a great medium used to help facilitate our aim.

- Uplifting music (drumming, southern gospel, praise & worship, spirituals, folk, Latin (Cuban, Puerto Rican, Brazilian, etc.) Espiritisimo music, etc. Whatever music you choose, it should be able to be played aloud to encourage dancing and/or contemplation.

- Last but not least a picture or image of Osar, the archetype for resurrection. The choice is yours as to what image you would like to use. If you feel comfortable using an Afrocentric Jesus, do so because again you are in control.

Once you have completed building the het for your aakhu. You can now build a het for your netcharu. I recommend that you should build the het for your netcharu after working with your aakhu, and receiving the inspiration to do so.

Het Netcharu and Het Aakhu

To build a spiritual house to honor both classes of spirits, you just need to add a second tier to the previous spiritual house. This should only be done if you feel inspired and only then, because working with the netcharu attracts a lot of spiritual energy. You will know when the netcharu are ready to manifest themselves to you, when you all of a sudden get an inspiration out of the blue to purchase a shelf or some type of structure to put in your space for them. Until that time, continue to work with your het aakhu.

If you feel inspired, the netcharu may also want sacred space established for them. If this is the case you can purchase either a picture or a figurine of the netchar. Although the netcharu are Kamitic in origin, it is not necessary that you have a Kamitic image. Any image can be used to represent the netcharu because they are linked with nature. It is important to understand that because Kamta is a heroic path, all of the netcharu (both male and female) are seen as being warriors since they fought against Set in their own way. Strength is not just about physical prowess but spiritual power as well. So don't be surprise if your female netcharu like Oset, Maat and even the lovely Nebhet request to have "paint" put on their arms or backs to symbolize ritual scarring a sign of strength. This is simply your aakhu manifesting themselves through the netcharu, to encourage you to learn about your culture. But, the netcharu are spirits of resistance against evil, so where they stand since most warriors don't sit (where their sacred house will be placed) will depend upon the role they play in your life.

There are however, a couple of rules that apply when constructing space for the netchar and they are (1) if you are using a picture it should never be placed on the floor but always hung up along the wall (preferably in a frame). The second rule is that whatever image you use. It should be treated with respect as if the netchar is present within it.

After creating space for your aakhu the first netchar you want to create sacred space is Npu. The netcharu Npu and his aakhu are very tricky in nature. Since Npu is very fickle, he will move his het from place to place until he feels comfortable. When he finally settles (usually behind or near a front door, though not always), because wherever the Opener of the Way stands, Set is usually not too far behind. So, Hruaakhuti stands alongside Npu and to ensure that balance is maintained and Maat[17] stands with Hruaakhuti. The het for Npu should be accommodating for Hruaakhuti and Maat's aakhu. If not, Hruaakhuti will always be trying to move next to Npu and Maat will try to keep them both out of trouble.

---

[17] Sometimes if there is space created for Djahuti, Maat will want to stand with him.

Typically in the Afro-Diaspora Hruaakhuti's space consists of an iron cauldron but this is not necessary. If you are fortunate to have some strong elderly men around, they may have a space for Hruaakhuti already established. There may be a bucket with tools and rusty lose nails and screws or, even a tool shed out back. These are all Hruaakhuti's dwellings. A simple space could be to take an iron chain and arrange it in a circle. Then put an image of a hawk inside, the symbolism is simple, Hruaakhuti is oversees and protector those who live the maa aankh.

Maat is very fond of Native American imagery due to them wearing feather headdresses. Often times when you feel the urge or are drawn to Native American icons it is an aakhu that may be trying to get you to acknowledge this part of your heritage. Also, this aakhu may assist in helping you to learn about Maat. Again follow your intuition, ask your *ba* as to which icon would help attract Maat to you.

Once Npu's space has been built, you may have some netcharu that will like to share the space with your aakhu. Generally speaking, netcharu like Osar, Djahuti and Sokar, since each corresponds to a different form of rebirth and transformation through knowledge, wisdom or spiritual power, will inspire you to place their image of them on the space for your aakhu. Remember, if you have a picture of the netcharu they should be placed above your aakhu (preferably hung on the wall) or the picture should be larger than that of your aakhu, to give the impression that they are watching over the aakhu.

Unless you have a special connection with Osar and Djahuti these netcharu usually do not make them selves known or their sacred space will require very little. This is because they are truly in KAMTA. The spaces that I have seen created for them are usually very beautiful and reflective of their high spiritual energy. This is why they are commonly represented on the altar for the aakhu. Usually, only Osar and Sokar descends from the higher realms of KAMTA and has a separate space to remind us of the transformative power of the Rau. Djahuti it can be said likes to spend his time staring into the heavens.

Hru and his aakhu generally prefers to sit or stand alone in high places, so he likes his het to be on bookshelves where he can see everything from afar and one must come to see him. Other times he will stand on the floor but this it is only temporary.

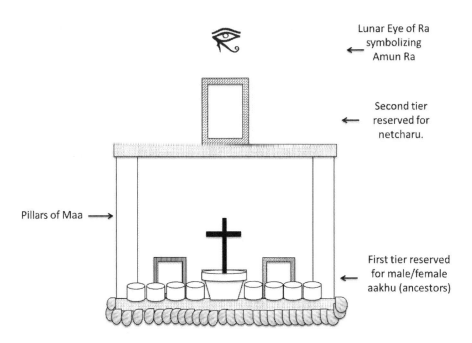

Lunar Eye of Ra symbolizing Amun Ra

Second tier reserved for netcharu.

Pillars of Maa →

First tier reserved for male/female aakhu (ancestors)

Two Story Kamta Het (Spiritual House/Altar)

As a word of caution, never erect Hru's het near Hruaakhuti because these are two different aspects of fire. These two netcharu work great together for very short terms goals like defeating Set, but if they stand together for too long. They will fight each other because they are always trying to outdo one another, thereby giving power to Set.

Oset's and her aakhu depending upon circumstances will either like to sit with Osar or usually with her sister Nebhet. If this is the case, her het should be placed where there is water like the bathroom or kitchen, which is a reminder to continue to look, continue nourishing and continuing to be devoted to Osar.

Nebhet and her aakhu, like Oset, enjoy having a het in the kitchen and bathroom but since she has a tendency to be a little lazy. If the kitchen or bathroom becomes filthy in any way, she will retreat to the bedroom. Where she might stand or invite Hru to enter (Hint: the two are said to be lovers). If the bedroom becomes filthy, she will leave your dwelling and will have to be swayed with sweet things to return.

Just like the netcharu sometimes have preference on being with the aakhu, there are times when the aakhu will want to be near specific netcharu. You may be inspired to place a photo of an aakhu near your Npu because maybe the aakhu needs assistance crossing over or needs to help another aakhu over. You may have an aakhu that wants to sit with Djahuti in order to better assist you in solving a problem. You may also be in a store and a particular figurine of an African, Native American, Gypsy, etc. catches your eye and prompts you to buy it. Then when you take the piece home it may want to sit or stand on your space with the aakhu or with a particular netcharu. No one really knows (without going into trance) what really happens in KAMTA – the Black Lands. All I know is that there is a system of some sort that exists regardless of what anyone chooses to believe. Rather than try to figure it out, it helps to simply embrace it and work it to your benefit.

Please note that I am speaking spiritually or metaphorically. These spirits are always around us but in order to see them in our life. We have to see them for what they are, which is invisible energies. The more we identify with them and see them as being forces. The easier it will be to detect when they are near and when something has gone awry.

In case you're wondering why am I being so vague in my description it is because I am trying to encourage you to follow your *ba*. I shouldn't have to spell everything out to you. If I do, then you are not listening to your *ba* because it is your *ba* that approves of everything that you. So, please note that the above were given as guidelines. The only hard-core rules you need to follow are the ones given above, which are do not place living people on your space for obvious reasons. And, second always keep your *hets* clean to avoid attracting aapepu.

For the Restricted Practitioner

Now, the beauty of this practice is that you do not have to have an elaborate space to honor your aakhu and netcharu. If you are not allowed because of limited space or some other circumstances to construct a large sacred space, you can do so by using a small representation. This is how our ancestral knowledge survived the treacherous Middle Passage. Remember, Oset and Nebhet left little small trinkets all over the place that became altars for Osar. This became possible because the netcharu have transcended the ordinary realm and have merged with nature. Consequently, if prying eyes prevents you from erecting a desirable space for Oset, a conch shell, clamshell or image of a mermaid will work just fine. An elephant with trunk raised can be used to represent Hru. Even a pebble found on the crossroad or in a wooded area can be used for Npu. A white stone can be used to symbolize the knowledge, strength and the backbone of Osar, and so on.

Typical Offerings

Because we are talking about spiritual work, it is customary to give spirits offerings in exchange for their assistance. Even though the aakhu and netcharu do not have a physical body, spirits are still able to consume the essence of things, which gives them energy. Keeping in mind that the KAMTA is a mirror reflection of TASETT, the following is a list of typical offerings and declarations to be said when making the offering:

- Alcoholic beverages –The most common alcoholic beverage is rum due to the Afro – Caribbean influence, followed by beer, whiskey, champagne and wine. When alcohol is not abused it is drank to celebrate life. It is offered to the spirits for enjoyment while asking that they help you enjoy life in return. Only a shot glass or small teacup of alcohol is offered to excite the spirits. You don't want to get your spirits drunk! Declaration: "I offer you this beer (rum, whiskey, etc.) for your enjoyment pleasure and ask in return that you give me pleasurable things in life."

- Candies – are given in the physical world for two reasons that I can recall, to either make a child be quiet or because you have bad or stale breath. Candies are offered to the spirits when there seems to be no movement, no progress and things seem stagnant, and while asking that the same way you refresh them they refresh your life. Declaration: "I offer you these candies and ask in return you not let my growth become stagnant. "

- Candles – typically white candles are offered to provide spirits with light and warmth, while asking that they give you light and warmth in return. Declaration: "I offer you this candle for light and warmth and ask in return you give me light and warmth into my life."

- Coffee – is offered to keep the spirits alert while asking that they help you to stay alert and aware. Never offer diluted coffee with sugar unless you want them to go to sleep on you. To be aware is not only to be conscientious about your surroundings but conscientious as to what is going into your spirit. Declaration: "I offer you this coffee and ask that you help me to always be aware."

- Food – all food especially fruit symbolizes bounty and it is offered to provide nourishment, while asking that they provide you with the food you needed to live in the physical land. Never salt your food that is being offered to the spirits. Salt repels spirits. Declaration: "I offer you this food for your nourishment, and ask that you give me food for my nourishment."

- Floral Incense and Floral Colognes/Perfumes – (like Florida Water, sandalwood, etc.) are offered to help the spirits attract pleasing things in the spirit land, while asking that they help attract pleasing things to you in the physical land. Declaration: "I offer you cologne (perfumes, incense, etc.), to attract beauty, and ask that you help me attract uplifting energies into my life."

- Flowers – are a common offering that is offered to give beauty to the spirits, while asking that they bring beauty to you in the physical land. Traditionally white flowers are offered but the spirits like vibrant things. Yellow flowers are also a very good flower to offer. The rule with flowers is that because they die quickly they should be either quickly replaced or not placed on the altar. Declaration: "I offer you these flowers to attract beauty, and ask that you help me attract beautiful things in my life."

- Money – is offered so that the spirits will have money to spend in the spiritual land, while asking that they give you money in the physical land. I learned from talking to a Vietnamese friend of mine that in folk Taoism many Asian families burn special money called *Hell Money* (fake money printed to look like real currency) for this purpose. This ritual is apparently very successful because you rarely see any impoverished people of Asian descent in the United States. Declaration: "I offer you money and ask that you give me money in return."

- Sweets – cakes and other pastries are only offered to help the spirits get through the difficult areas in the spirit land, while asking that they assist us getting through the bitter areas in the physical land. Declaration: "I offer you these pastries (cake) for your enjoyment and in return you assist me in life."

- Tobacco – tobacco is an herb adopted from our contact with the Native Americans. It is strong herb that assists in clearing the way for peace, which is why it was an essential element in the Peace Pipe Ceremony. If you do not smoke cigarettes when offered you may immediately sense the power of this herb when the cigar is burned and offered in this manner. Puffs of smoke are given to give peace to the spirits, while asking that they clear a way for peace in the physical land. Only three puffs of smoke are necessary. If you find that after several minutes smoke is still being drawn from the cigar, it could indicate that the aakhu and netcharu are near. Declaration: "I offer you this smoke so that it clears a path of peace for you and I ask that in return you clear a path of peace for me."

- Water – is offered to quench your spirits thirst, while asking that they don't allow you to become spiritually thirsty. For this reason, never allow your glasses on your aakhu het to go dry. Whenever you see the water has evaporated, refill it to the rim. Declaration: "I offer you this water to quench your thirst and ask in return you never allow me to become spiritual thirsty."

Honoring the Aakhu and Netcharu

To open communication, assuming your glasses on the aakhu altar are filled. The aakhu are always honored before the netcharu, because they are closest to us and they are the spirits that most of us remembered when they were alive. The aakhu are the backbone of this practice, so the connection to them is far easier to come by then it is with the netcharu. In order to properly honor an aakhu they must have been physically deceased at least for six months. Communication begins by first:

1. Knocking three times on the floor. This is to signal that you are entering into KAMTA. You can also ring a bell or a maraca.

2. Say the Lord's Prayer. (The Lord's Prayer is being used because most people are familiar with it and do not know how to properly

80

pray with a strong conviction. It creates a strong thought-form that discourages aapepu from entering into your space. It also helps to put you in the right frame of mind).

3. Thank your aakhu by saying a simple prayer like "Thank you for your strength, wisdom, knowledge and power."

4. Next light a white candle and an uplifting incent like frankincense while saying, "I offer you this candle and this incense for light, warmth and to attract beauty. I ask in return you give me light and warmth into my light, and help me attract uplifting energies into my life." Every offering should be presented with a declaration in order to get your *ba*, *ab* and *sahu* to work together. If inspired to offer cigar smoke. Blow three puffs of cigar smoke on the altar and say, "I offer you this smoke so that it clears a path of peace for you and I ask that in return you clear a path of peace for me." If offering a shot of rum you say, "I offer you this rum for your enjoyment pleasure and ask in return that you give me pleasurable things in life." If you do not have a het for the netcharu you can end this ritual by simply saying "Thank you."

5. If you have a het for the netcharu. For each het you have created you must honor that netchar. If you only have Npu then you must honor Npu because that netchar has chosen to make him or her known in your life. If you on the other hand, have Npu and Hru you have to honor both of them, and so on. Listed below are basic declarations I used for honor the netcharu. This is combined with the declaration for the offerings. Simply light a white birthday candle and say the following declaration:

   • Osar: "Thank you Osar for peace, prosperity and wisdom."

   • Oset: "Thank you Oset for love, nurturance and protection."

   • Npu: "Npu, Guardian spirit of us all. Thank you for Opening the Way and guiding me safely to my destination."

- Hru: "Thank you Hru for success and victory over the enemy."

- Hruaakhuti: "Thank you for protecting me from danger seen and unseen."

- Maati "Thank you for bringing balance, order and justice into my life."

- Djahuti: "Thank you for repairing my Eye, so that I can see clearly."

- Nebhet: "Thank you Nebhet for love, harmony and happiness."

- Sokar: "Thank you Sokar for health, strength and rebirth."

6. Next turn on the uplifting music of your choice or if possible play an instrument for your spirits like the drums, flute, horn, whatever the case. Go with the flow. Afterwards, either stand or sit (in a straight back chair with feet on the ground – never crossed legged) before your altar.

7. When you have finished, if you do not have anything that you want to discuss, then simply thank your spirits for their assistance and allow the candle to burn out.

8. If you do need help around an issue you are facing, ask for assistance or help. The easiest way to communicate with your netcharu and aakhu is by talking to them aloud about your problems as if you were talking to your best friend. And then listen to the thoughts that your aakhu and netcharu put into your mind. Remember, because you have an *ab* (spiritual heart/soul-self) the spirits are compelled to listen to you and to try to assist you in solving your problems.

9. Simply state aloud what the problem is or what you would like to discuss. Then sit, enter into Twilight and wait for a response. Although medium-ship often occurs at this point, it is not encouraged. Note that the answer does not have to be audible or

melodramatic. Just watch the thoughts that enter into your awareness and follow your intuition. At this time you may be inspired to move, dance, and draw or read a particular passage from a book. You may have epiphanies, flashback or a recollection of deceased family member. These are signs that your ancestors are trying to communicate to your *ba*. You may be taken to a distant land or something that occurred during your childhood might be brought back to your awareness. Whatever the case do not fight it by giving too much thought to it. Simply follow your *ba* intuition because the spirits are trying to show you something. Write down whatever comes to mind if this is not too difficult for you and does not distract you.

I have found that a lot of times spirit communication occurs when you are not focused on anything or, you are busy doing something totally unrelated to the subject. For instance, like while watching television, driving to work, talking to a complete stranger, etc. This usually occurs because our *sahu* is too connected to the subject matter at hand, so you find yourself trying to address an issue but are worried about the outcome. You find it too hard to keep your mind clear. When this occurs simply state what you want and leave it in your netcharu and aakhu's hands. One of the best ways to do this is to write out what you want and be descriptive as possible. Then burn it, thank your spirits and go watch television, play a game, wash the dishes or something to force your *sahu* to leave the subject alone.

10. When you have finished, thank your spirits and allow the candle to burn out. Take the answers that you have jotted down and see if what you have been told is true. Note the way that the messages came to you because this usually will be the way that your aakhu and netcharu will communicate to you in the future. This should be repeated at least once a week at the time when you least likely to be disturbed. Some say that Monday or Friday is the best day to perform this ceremony. Personally, I have found that Saturday works best because it is a powerful day for renewing charms.

In time when you have finished, standing in front of your spirits should feel like you are in the presence of a spiritual tribunal. Understand that these are your spiritual allies. They are not deities but your personal guardian angels and spirit guides, so treat them as you would treat your best friend. When you want something, ask them to help you get it. When you receive your assistance need to pay them for their help by giving them an offering.

Your Spiritual Tribunal

Just like when Hru stood before the tribunal and defended his case against Set. The idea is that you are doing the same. Before you are your spiritual helpers and any time you need spiritual assistance. You can present your problem to them and ask for guidance revolving around the issue.

In time as you develop a stronger rapport with your aakhu and netcharu you can begin offering them certain food items that they are fond with. When offering food items never allow the food to stay before the spirit and spoil because it will attract the negative energies. If offering food to the aakhu never salt the food, this repels all spirits and when offering shots of rum or any other beverage (including water); it should be enough to last throughout the whole week. If for instance, you find that you are having some unusual difficulties and feel like there are some walls built up against you in your life. You might want to check your mason jar of rum to Hruaakhuti. He and his aakhu may have consumed the rum offering to avert certain evils in your life and may require a little bit more.

Now, if you are unable to offer the above offerings for whatever reason. Do not fret. Understand this is all about energy and the typical offerings are the ways energy is given, but it is not the only way. Any time you give attention to anything you give it energy. Everything that exists is composed of energy, the difference being that physical things move at a much slower rate, while spirits move at a fast pace. So, you can give anything energy just by talking to it. This is one of the significance of having an *ab*, which is how miracles (or magic) are performed and why Moses was so exalted by his people. If you can't give a particular offering because you can't afford it or it is not available at the time, tell your spirits. If they want it they will make it accessible. Remember, you are in control and you shouldn't feel uncomfortable in anything that you do. If you do, then it is not genuine.

Chapter 6:
Finding the Truth and Your Truth

Now that we have discussed the nature of the human being and how when our *ab* awareness is introverted, our unlimited *ba* can provide our limited *sahu* with a solution to any problem; we can now discuss how to constructively use this spiritual science to create positive change. Then we discussed how our netcharu and aakhu speak to us through our ba, while the aapepu usually appeal to us through our sahu. We need to discuss how this system works by familiarizing you with the Maa – the Absolute Truth – and your maa – personal truth.

You could have learned how to enter into trance, build hets (spiritual houses) and everything up to this point, but you will not be able to precede any further without Maa. It is only by learning and dedicating your life to living according to the Maa that you are able to grow, because Maa is what fuels this practice and is the basis of the maa aankh.

Before we begin, understand that you do not have to be perfect. In fact, you will have problems, which is totally understandable. The reason you have been brought here to this point, right now, is to receive spiritual assistance in overcoming the problems you have in your life. That's right. You have been Called and your netcharu and aakhu are willing to assist you in your rebirth (total change of consciousness), but once you start walking down this path. There is no turning back. I am not telling you this to frighten you. I am telling you this because Maa is about adapting and changing, which means you cannot continue to be the same individual you were from beginning to end. You have to change your behavior, character, and personality and strive to be a better individual. This is because contrary to what our contemporary society may believe. There are certain things our aakhu and netcharu will not tolerate. If you try to pervert their way, they will leave you and allow you to attract the wrong elements and situations to you. This is not cruel, you must remember the netcharu and aakhu vibrate at a higher frequency and can descend from higher realms upon their choosing, because their *ab* continues to survive. If you engage in perverted actions and behaviors this changes the frequency they are on and two things can't occupy the same space at the same time.

You will therefore, reach a point by following this path where you will be required to make a decision to stay the same way and continue experiencing obstacles and setbacks, or choose to move ahead and learn how to overcome these tribulations by conquering the anxiety, fears and worries of your *sahu*. These are the moments it will come to you that you need to make maa aankh and when you do so with serious intent. You will not break the oath and return to your old habits and ways.

Guilt: The Greatest Kamitic Sin

I am not a trained medical physician, psychologist, sociologist, licensed theologian or clergyman. I like you am a truth seeker and after studying various religious faiths. I have concluded that if most people did not have a set of laws or rules in place. They would commit a number of heinous acts. I will not bore you with my beliefs as to why people commit evil, such as is it because of ignorance, sin, etc. I will leave this for you to decide. The fact is however, that people will commit evil resulting in them having a heavy feeling of guilt upon their *ab* (spiritual heart).

Guilt is a horrible and powerful energy to be hauling around from place to place. When you feel guilty of doing anything, it boggles your mind and prevents you from advancing mentally, physically and spiritually, because it is a safety feature that is linked to our *ab*. It is one of the features that distinguish human beings from animals. Notice if you will that animals don't feel any remorse for killing another animal. A lion for instance, is not remorseful for killing its prey. It does what it needs to do in order to feed. Most human beings on the other hand are remorseful whenever they harm another and this is because as children. We felt and saw the consequences of our actions and behaviors. Again, I said that this is for most people. There are a few individuals in our society that feel no remorse and this we will see in the future is because their *ab* has not evolved past the animal moment of the maa aankh. These individuals (such as serial killers, terrorists, etc.) are known as beast men and women because they are blinded by their passions of hate, lust, power and are associated with Set.

Returning back to our subject, the purpose of guilt is to help us to right the wrong or simply to restore balance. This is the reason it is common courtesy for you to apologize when you have wrong another, and, say "Thank you" whenever someone offers you a favor or gives you a gift, and so on. These are all ways removing guilt, so that you don't feel like you have been taken advantage of or have taken advantage of another.

As you can imagine, this is how the very first principles of religion began. Early gatherers said "Thank you (to somebody)" for the nuts, berries and fruits that they found in the wilderness. Early hunters to remove the remorse from killing another living being said "Thank you" and apologized to the animal they killed that would provide their family with sustenance. The feeling of guilt was lessened or removed through these ritual actions, which is the reason why today people continue to say grace over their meals. But this energy never totally went away. Guilt and remorse stayed and it inspired early hunters and gatherers so that they didn't abuse the land or savagely kill animals, thereby destroying the ecosystem.

This is the purpose of guilt and remorse, but due to a lack of understanding on spiritual science. A lot of religious groups have used guilt and remorse in a negative manner, by claiming that if you don't follow a certain commandment, law, set of rules, a particular religious leader, etc. That you are going to be punished by God. This is why there are so many people that claim to believe in God who are committing heinous acts against their own brethren. Remember, guilt and remorse are supposed to make you feel bad when an imbalance or transgression has been made. So, if an individual does not feel any guilt or remorse for bombing a religious center (church, temple, mosque, etc.), persecuting or terrorizing others just because they don't share the same beliefs. What makes them different from an animal? Not much as you can see.

So, most (if not all) laws were originally created not to keep God's commandments, but to ease the burden of carrying around guilt. The reason (as I am sure you have figured out by now) is because it is guilt and remorse that prevents us from fulfilling our destiny as human beings, thereby keeping us from connecting to God. Understand we are all God's creatures and are intimately connected to God. Technically speaking none of us can be disconnected from God, but out of all of creation. Only human beings have an *ab*, which gives us the right to choose to follow either our animal instincts associated with our *sahu* or, our *ba* that connects us directly to divine. This means that if you have no remorse for the wrong you are doing then you are following your instincts just like an animal and not choosing to follow your *ba*. Therefore, the real

87

purpose of laws and commandments is to prevent us from carrying the burden of guilt on our *ab*, so that we can connect to our *ba*.

The problem is that most people don't understand this because they don't understand what is truth or Absolute Truth. Most people believe that the Absolute Truth is written in some book, which is why we often hear people (especially religious leaders) say when speaking about commandments and laws that "the Truth" will set you free. The thing is that if it was the Absolute Truth it should be the truth not one day out of the week but all of the time, for everyone and everybody. This we see is not the case. For instance, just think about the commandment "Thou shalt not kill." A great commandment that works for preventing people from harming another, but we see that it couldn't be the Absolute Truth because this commandment it is not applicable during wartime or when it comes to protecting yourself and your family. Why isn't applicable? It is because life is not black and white. If it were, when people go to school they would either pass with a 100% or fail, no in between, which sounds absolutely ridiculous. This is why the Kamitic philosophers placed so much emphasis on understanding the Absolute Truth.

Understanding the Maa and Your Personal Maa

Truth in the Kamitic language is called Maa, which as we saw in previous chapters means "truth, balance, order, justice, righteousness, and law," but it also "means to see" and "to measure." The Kamitic philosophers defined the Absolute Truth as Maa because they understood that the Truth is objective, meaning the Absolute Truth is not influenced by an individual's feelings or opinions. It is based upon facts. To understand this position it must be acknowledge that we all have different affiliations, backgrounds, different experiences and thereby different beliefs. It is these differences that we all have, which makes us unique but it also creates confusions among ourselves because it is hard for us to agree upon the same thing. What may be good for one person may be bad for another because of an individual's cognizance. Take for instance the concept of death. We all know that regardless of our belief, culture, etc. that everything physically dies. This is a truth that no one can dispute. What happens after death, do we go to heaven, purgatory or hell? Do we wait for judgment, etc. are all related to one's personal beliefs, understandings, ideas and experience? So, in order to have truth there has to be something that we can all agree upon all the time, anytime and everywhere. When we can all agree upon the same thing, regardless of our affiliations, background, etc. We have a law, a balanced equation based upon observing cause and effects, the Truth or Maa.

For instance, an apple thrown into the sky falls back down to the ground because of gravity. It doesn't matter where on the planet we throw an apple or anything up in the sky. It will come back down because of the law of gravity. This is Maa. The fact that we all need oxygen in order to breathe and live and on the planet, and the same air that fills our lungs also fills the lungs of animals, our family, friends and even our adversary. Is a proven fact that God is not bias and doesn't favor one over another. This is Maa, but as you can see it takes some maturity to be able to truly arrive at this understanding.

There is the Maa, which is the Absolute Truth that appears on the maa aankh, and then there is the *maa* – one's balance, personal truth or way. The difference between the two is that the latter pertains to one's personal cognizance. One's *maa* is as Papa told me is their *la manera* or what works for them based upon their experience. For this reason, one's maa is spelled in lowercase to make the distinction between one's personal truth and Maa – the Truth. When someone tells you that they are telling the truth you have to determine are they telling you about their maa or the Maa. If they say "That everything that goes up must come down," this is Maa, but if they say, "You have to belong to this group, in order to get something accomplished." You know that they are speaking from their maa, which is usually their opinion. Usually, you can tell when someone is telling you their opinion because you will hear the word "I".

What is sin? Sin is anything that perverts your *ab* awareness. This is why every tradition has a set of principles that are taught to help people understand the power of God and how to work with it constructively. Unfortunately, as stated previously the lack of spiritual sciences has led many people to believe that these principles are supposed to be a set of rules that dictate what you can and cannot do. If you obey the rules then it is believed that God will reward you. If you disobey these rules or sin you will be punished by God. This is nonsense. For instance, the commandment for killing should read, "(Ideally) thou shalt not kill" not saying that you cannot and will never kill. This is because if you eat vegetables, meat or grains, you technically speaking have killed. If you chopped down wood to build a house, you have killed. Can you see and feel the difference? When you adopt a different perspective and see

89

everything as a living being. It gives you a greater awareness, but it also makes you more conscientious about your actions and behaviors. If you see this congratulation, you have just stepped on the Maa.

I hope by now you see that God is not a cruel and tyrannical Deity. God does not reward or punish anyone. All undesirable experiences are the consequences of actions and reactions and not because God is punishing you. This is why the Maa is symbolized as a vertical line on the maa aankh. You will notice that the maa connects the Ra above with Amun Ra below together, because it is all about Cause and Effect, remaining in balance and seeing the whole picture. People who don't understand this and believe that God is a vengeful Deity have no experience with meditative practices and don't understand the Alpha state of trance. In fact, most of the evil that is done in this world is by people whose *ab* is at the Ra moment of the maa aankh. The Ra moment you will recall is the point of adventure and where trouble starts, because our awareness is extroverted at a highly active and emotional state. Later, we will see that this particular moment corresponds to the archetype Set, the Kamitic devil.

Spiritual principles were created for those who want to improve their life by shifting their *ab* awareness to their *ba* and away from the *sahu*, to create miraculous change. To do this we must first learn how to rid our *ab* of stain of guilt and remorse.

Removing Guilt

As I stated in the beginning of this discourse, I am not a trained medical physician, psychologist, sociologist, licensed theologian or clergyman. I say that because I want you to understand that we have all experienced or have done some things that we may not be proud of, which is a part of life. This is because we are not perfect. If we were perfect we would not be here, so the first thing to do to remove guilt is to:

1. Recognize what the transgression is that makes you feel guilt.
2. Forgive yourself for committing the transgression. Understand a lot of when we do wrong it is because we simply didn't know any better. If you had known better you could have acted in another way, so forgive yourself.

3. Forgive the other individual (or individuals) that you have wronged. If it is possible try to apologize to the individual in person and make whatever means to restore the Maa. If they are no longer living, pray to God and then imagine individual. Then offer them your deepest apologies and ask that God forgive you.
4. If you were wronged by another forgive them for not knowing any better, rather they are aware of their actions or not. If you need some help, ask Nebertcher for strength in doing so.
5. To ensure that the guilt does not return. You have to make maa aankh, which is "Swear an oath to live truth." There are many ways to do this but the whole idea is that you make a commitment to God, your ancestors and yourself, not to commit the same transgression[18]. The simplest way is to imagine standing on the maa aankh, while placing your right hand on your heart. Then you state aloud that you promise not to make the same transgression. Now, only make maa aankh if you are serious about growth and change, which signals to the universe that you are for real.

These are some simple ways of clearing your *ab*. Note that if the guilt is really strong, you might want to consider seeing a professional. Whatever the case, you need to deal with this issue because if not, the guilt will tear you down. It will ride you hard and you will constantly be thinking about the individual that you either wronged or wronged you, and thereby not able to progress in life.

Another way to ensure that the guilt is removed is to pray daily. I cannot overstate the effectiveness of the *Lord's Prayer*, because it is a very general, simple yet powerful prayer that can be prayed by anyone regardless of their beliefs. When prayed daily it makes a very effective way of removing guilt before it becomes too strong. The other way to keep guilt at bay is through the Seven Codes of Maa.

---

[18] A similar type of ritual is done in most churches but the guilt usually returns because the pious is told to cast their entire guilty burden upon Jesus, and then they return to their hellish ways. Spiritual growth occurs, thereby removing guilt, when we see the errors of our ways. So, in lieu of giving one's burdens to Jesus they should also ask for forgiveness from those whom they wronged. This makes for an effective ritual.

The Seven Codes of Maa: Kamitic Ethics

Since guilt is hardwired into our being, we need a set of principles to help us keep from staining our *ab*. The purpose of these principles is not to justify our negative actions and behaviors, but to help us make changes at will with jeopardizing our *ab*. The purpose of the Seven Codes of Maa, is to simply remind you how you are supposed to go about creating change. They are based upon the principles of nature and since nothing is nature is static and is subject to change. The Seven Codes can be bent, while others can be broken. You simply have to learn which applies to you.

The following seven principles, which I have adapted from other resources and my experience, are my interpretation of the principles of Maa. I have written a brief commentary about each, called What You Need to Remember to Work the Rau, to remind you of the key points of the principle that you need to remember.

Code #1: Maa is Truth & Is Based Upon Perspective

In the West, most people believe that Truth can be found in books, so we study religion, mysticism, metaphysics, philosophy, etc. in search of the Absolute Truth, so that we can make sense of the world around us. Some of us will even blindly follow in the footsteps of others because no one has told us. That the Absolute Truth does not exist in a book, it is what we make it. This is a little hard to understand because it is assumed that one solution should address us all, but we are different.

We are all unique in our own way because we have different backgrounds and have had different experiences. Our uniqueness means that we have been created for a specific purpose that is only known to God. Some of us were created to be educators, some engineers, some musicians, and some physicians and so on. We all have our own individual purposes and in order to accomplish our destinies there are certain life experiences that we need. Some of us need to fall from grace in order for us to see the beauty of the Divine, while others have to rise from the streets to affluence in order to see the Divine. We are all unique beings and we all have different needs, so what makes people think that we are all supposed to have the same beliefs, creed, affiliations, etc. What works for one person doesn't necessarily mean that it will work for another the exact same way. Truth is all about perspective. Absolute truth is whatever works to bring you into the fold of the Divine. If it brings you eternal peace and eternal happiness, then it is truth for you because it works for you. Note however, that I said eternal peace and eternal happiness, which can only come from the Divine.

What You Need to Remember to work the Rau #1:
See the Drinking Gourd as Half Empty or Half Full

This is a lesson I learned from reading and studying the life of the Civil Rights leader Malcolm X. Malcolm X it should be remembered was able to do God's will because of Islam. This is why it is said that every religion has a piece of the Absolute Truth. So everything that we do will lead us to heaven either directly or indirectly, because it comes from God. Eventually scientist in their quest to understand the universe will too find God. Their atheistic perspective is needed in order for them to make the discoveries that they have made thus far. Nothing happens by coincidence, so it is important when working the Spirit not to take anything that you can see physically as being Absolute Truth. Look beyond the physical and learn to see the flip side of every situation. This will give you a great advantage in life because it will allow you to focus all the time on solutions and not the problems, thus making you a co-creator of life.

Note I didn't say you weren't supposed to acknowledge that problems exist. Yes, acknowledge it but afterwards move on. Sitting around dwelling and sulking on how a problem occurred or illness happened only gives more energy to the problem at hand. Remember, it is your thoughts that spark your emotions, which motivates your actions and behaviors. So, the more you think about a problem, an illness, or whatever troubles you. The larger it becomes and harder it will be for you to find a solution to it.

So decide right now to either to see the glass or drinking gourd as being half empty or half full. Because this world – TASETT – is never going to give you everything you want or need. Life has never been fair and it will never be so long as you put your stake in what you can physically see. You have to learn to put your faith in the invisible and know that all that you desire will come to past when you change your perspective and focus your attention on your goal.

93

Code #2: Maa is Balance & Is Limited By the Mind

If life is whatever you make it, then there are no limits to what you can become because everything is based upon the Maa – Divine Order of Cause and Effect. Unfortunately, most ideas about Maa usually are about injustices and of someone wronging another, then being punished. This belief stems from stories of a vengeful deity reprimanding wrongdoers for committing sin. The truth is that God does not reprimand people for their actions. As I stated above if you tossed up a rock and it fell down. Hit you on the head and knocked you unconscious for a few minutes. Would you say that God punished you for throwing a rock in the air? No. You would say that it was the law of gravity that caused the rock to fall and you didn't get out of the way of where it was falling. Right? The next time when you throw a rock in the air you will watch where it is falling or at least throw it at a safe distance so that you are able to catch it. This is Maa. You learned from the consequences of your actions. You now have a full picture and clear understanding of the Divine Order of Cause and Effects in regards to throwing rocks.

In the above example, you see your beliefs changed as a result of your experience, which means that it is our beliefs based upon our experience that prevent us from seeing the full picture. We created these beliefs in order for us to physically survive. We created these limitations in order for us to understand our physical reality, but these beliefs cannot assist us in tapping into the Spirit because the Spirit is Infinite. In order to tap into the Spirit we have to understand that the Spirit is not bound by time and space. This means that when a thought is impressed upon the Spirit. It has the ability to inspire the appropriate action to manifest whatever we want.

What You Need to Remember to work the Rau #2:
The Sky is the Limit

Do you know the reason why people don't know how the pyramids were built? It is because Western thinkers place a limitation on themselves by believing that the ancients did not possess the technology to create such an edifice, by labeling the people as primitive. They continue to do this in regards to other life forms in our universe. They send droids to other planets to prove their belief that there are no other life forms that exists. This phenomenon is known as perceptual blindness and Daniel Simons of

94

University of Illinois and Christopher Chabris of Harvard University conducted best-known study of it.

In the experiment, subjects were asked to watch a video and count the number of times a basketball is passed amongst two groups of people (wearing black and white t-shirts). While the video is playing, a woman in a guerilla suit carrying an umbrella walks through the scene. When the video is over the subjects are asked if they saw anything unusual. Out of the groups tested, half of them never saw the lady in the guerilla suit. The results of the experiment showed that while the subjects were focused on the challenging task of counting basketball passes. They failed to see even the most obvious images in front of them.

Being able to tap into the Spirit requires you being able to open your mind to the unlimited possibilities that exist. It is based upon the understanding that since the Spirit is Infinite and is connected to everyone and everything. Whatever we want out of life is limited only by what we believe.

Code #3: Maa is Harmony & Becomes What Attention is Focused On

Since the Rau is connected to everything. Everything that exists in the universe does so by harmonizing with the each other. This is what creates Maa and it is the reason why every natural system, like the ecosystem functions so perfectly. Think about that for a moment.

This means that everything in the universe from the quarks, electron, atoms, and molecules to all of the planets is composed of energy and exists in a vibratory state. The difference between the visible, physical matter and invisible, energy is that former is vibrating at a lower rate, whereas the latter is moving at an exceptionally high rate. The "things" we cannot see therefore has a greater influence upon us then the things we see. This principle besides explaining the difference between matter and energy also indicates that both are composites of the same whole. In other words, matter cannot exist without its polar energetic opposite, nor can energy exist without matter. Neither is more superior to the other. The material is needed for energy to express itself and energy is needed in order to give purpose to the material.

From a practical perspective, this means we are all spiritual beings composed of energy expressing ourselves through a physical body. The physical body is simply a vehicle for energy or the spirit to express itself through. As spiritual beings, wherever we generate a thought, it sparks our emotions, which motivates action and behavior yielding physical results. So, if you complain about how bad a situation is the situation will become progressively worse due to the energy you are putting into it. The same occurs when dealing with people. If you criticize a person about their negative behavior, usually the criticism only makes them act or behave out of anger, fear or spite. Try it for yourself. Let someone tell you what you can't do and watch your emotions flare as you go out of your way to prove them wrong.

The way to encourage constructive and positive action is by putting energy in what it is that you want. If you sincerely praise an individual for something you want they will be inspired to act and behave. I remember once there was a young man I knew, who would never clean up after himself, and do his chores and just expected people to do it for him. All he did was run the streets with his friends and he wondered why people were always on his back. No one could get him to take responsibility for himself. After talking to him a while about the things he enjoyed. I told him that if he would make sure that certain tasks were completed before hanging out with their friends. More people would respect him because he was demonstrating maturity. The next day this young man began to do his chores and clean up behind himself without anyone asking him to do so. By reinforcing his positive traits and their contributions to the whole, he managed to change his behavior.

To get what you want, we must learn to focus our *ab* awareness on what we want, and allow your *ba* to connect you to the Rau in order to make your wish a physical reality. That being said, one of the hardest lessons that you will have to learn is that you cannot change an individual by focusing your attention on them. You cannot make your boss a better person or make someone act right, because they have a *ba*, *ab* and *sahu* as well. There are lessons that they have to learn and goals in life they need to accomplish. At the same time, this doesn't mean that you have to put it with someone else's nonsense or take their abuse. You simply have to learn to put matters in your *ba's* hands, which is done by focusing on solutions and not the problems. And, when I say solutions, I mean the end result of what is desired.

For instance, I had some disruptive neighbors a married couple that would get drunk on the weekend and later on fight with each other. It was like clockwork, every weekend they would go through this same routine. Clearly, there were some domestic issues that they needed to address, but I couldn't tell these people they need to go get help. In fact, that might not have been the best option they needed. So, I put the request in my *ba's* hands by focusing on the house being quiet on the weekend in the evening. I maintained this focus and before long, it was quiet. No more waking up in the middle of the night hearing people argue and breaking things. Later, I found out that the couple was getting a divorce. They moved out of the house and later remarried.

What You Need to Remember to work the Rau #3:
Expect Something Wonderful and Not What Might Happen

One of the biggest dream and miracle killers is the dreaded "What if…" You have seen this before. It rears its ugly head every time you try to make some type of advancement. When you hear the dreaded, "What if…" it will either come from those closest to us like our family and friends, or from out of our own mouths. As I wrote in MAA AANKH, my most memorable experience with the dreaded what if demon is when I had purchased my first car. At the time I was in Florida and my mate and I had managed to scrounge up enough money to buy a used car, but we didn't have enough money to get car insurance. Like most people living paycheck-to-paycheck, I decided to purchase the car and when I got paid the next day. I would rush and get the car insurance but as I drove the car off the car lot. All I kept thinking was how I hope I don't get in a car accident. I mean I kept having what if scenarios pop up in my awareness that made me very anxious.

So, the next day I cautiously drove to work and as soon as I got my check, I cautiously drove to the check-cashing place and I was off to get some car insurance. Then, that's when it happened. On my way to get the insurance, while waiting in line to exit off the highway, all of a sudden a heavy spring rain came down. I remembered I looked up in the rear view mirror and there I saw a speeding pickup truck swerving and struggling to come to a stop. "This fool is going to hit me," I remembered saying to myself, "So let me cock my steering wheel." Sure enough, the young naval officer hit my car and totaled it. Funny thing, right after the accident, it stopped raining. In the end, the car was paid off by the other driver's insurance and I received a citation for not having any proof of insurance.

I have spent a number of years trying to figure out why exactly I had a car accident. I mean why when you expect things to go wrong they do. Why when it rains, does it pour or when you think things can't get any worse they do? It is because if you expect the worse, the worse will happen. I know it may sound unbelievable but I have seen it on every level. I have eaten something like a piece a chocolate and remember hearing my mother say when I was a teenager, "You're going to break out" and shortly after I see a pimple emerge on my face. It is because this is what I expected. It is because I expected it, my *sahu* responded accordingly. When I changed what I expected, my *sahu* stop responding as it had previously learned. For instance, to counter getting pimples after eating a piece of dark chocolate, I would drink a glass of water believing it would wash away the ill effects. I don't know where I got the idea from but whenever I ate a piece of dark chocolate and drank some water after it. I would not get any pimples. The reason this worked is because I taught my *sahu* to expect a different result from eating dark chocolate.

Now, before you go there, I am not advocating eating chocolate, sweets, candy, etc. What I am advocating is that you stop living your life in fear by remembering that the *sahu's* purpose is to help us physically survive. The *sahu* accomplishes this by relying upon its genetic and learned memories. When the *sahu* senses something is wrong, it reacts by sending a warning to our *ab* awareness as an unpleasant feeling of discomfort, pain, etc. because it is stressed. But, once you are aware of the warning you can temporary turn it off or ignore it. This is how athletes and those working in extreme conditions are able to continue to work under excruciating pain and horrendous conditions. Please note, that I said you can temporary turn it off, but do not do so for a long period of time. By this I mean, I don't sit and just continue to eat chocolate because this will have consequences too. Nor should athletes and those working in extreme conditions just continue to ignore the pain. You have to learn balance and this is how you can apply this principle.

So, whenever you receive an idea from your *ba* to apply for a new job, take a leap of faith to start a business, take a calculated risk to invest in a project, etc. and you find yourself asking or thinking, "What if…" Tell your *sahu* "But what is something wonderful happens as a result of taking this venture?" Tell and remind your *sahu* when it asks this question of the possibilities that will come from you embarking upon a new venture.

Code #4: Maa is Justice & Doing what is Right, Right Now

Hot and cold, fire and water, up and down, man and woman, etc. are polar opposites of the same coin expressing the duality of nature. Within every opposite is a small degree of its polar opposite, which is why every male species has feminine aspects and every female species also possesses to a certain degree masculine qualities.

This is important to understand because many people associate Maa with the Eastern concept of karma and the Western concept of original sin and generational curse. In Eastern philosophy, the belief is that the good actions you perform today will create good karma for you in your next life, while the bad actions and deeds you perform today will cause you to have bad karma in your next life. According to philosophy when one experiences good or bad karma it is because of something he or she did in his or her past life. Therefore, bad experiences are seen as the result of some karmic debt.

In the Western teachings, the belief is that the sins of a patriarch and/or an ancestor have inevitably doomed future generations. If the individual follows the tenets of the religion without question then they will be rewarded, but if they question or break any commandment they will be punished for sinning whether or not anyone observed them break the commandment or not.

Both of these philosophic approaches have produced an untold amount of guilt and worry that has prevented individuals from reaching their potential and accomplishing greatness. This is why even the great Christian sage Jesus in Matthew 6:34 taught his disciples against worry. It is because of the previous principles. Maa teaches that one cannot be responsible for the actions of others or what was done in the past, because the world is whatever we make it, which means it is not our past actions that determine our future. It is the thoughts, actions and choices that we make today that determine our future and who we are.

True karma is about cause and effect and it operates in the present, not in the past or the future. While we carry within us the genetic history and legacy of our ancestors, we have been given free will and it is because of our free will. We can either choose to follow old habits, outdated traditions and pathways or presently create new roads for others to follow. But change has never been easy and following the Maa is not always a piece of cake. We all must journey through the arid, horrendous, unfair Red Lands of TASETT in order to acquire spiritual power and wisdom to address the issues that we face. Why? Because how do you know what is good if you have never experienced the bad? How else can you fix a problem if you have never experienced or identified it? How can you enjoy a win if you have never lost? This is the reason we came to earth and it is the reason why the only way we can fulfill our destiny is by first experiencing adversity.

So it is important to act now in the present and not concern yourself with the past or the future. Everything that you have done and experienced has propelled you to this point in your life right now. Everything that you do presently brings you that much closer to your destiny. You can make a change in your life right now because what you do today is what determines your tomorrow.

Now that we have that out the way, we all know of someone that needs some fire put to his or her backside. You know that person no matter how nice, polite and ethical you are with them. They continue to kick in your door, step on your neck and disrespect you every chance they get. They are the ones we commonly call our enemies because they are bullies, deceitful neighbors, spiteful coworkers, hateful supervisors, vile landlords (or tenants), etc., etc. How do we deal with these individuals when it comes to the maa you ask? Are we supposed to just sit back and just let these individuals victimize our loved ones and us? No, we are not and if you do this is not Maa.

It amazes me how many people wonder in amazement of how God in the bible destroys the enemies of the Israelites and how people cheer for the victim, when they finally defeat the no good assailant. But, when it comes to them or their loved ones being abused personally, they just sit back and accept it because they heard that familiar scripture paraphrased, "...Vengeance is mine said the Lord." Remember, the Power of God is a blind force and unless asked it to intervene by our *ba* it will not act on our behalf. What this means is that if you allow yourself or loved ones to be abused, attacked, bullied, etc. It is going to continue until you reach your wits ends and have finally had enough.

I have seen time and time again, "spiritual people" just get handed their lunch and they just take the abuse because they are supposed to be "spiritual." When I ask why did they let that person step all over them and treat them like they were less than nothing. They tell me that it is because they don't want to mess up their "karma". When in truth the real reason they will not retaliate is because they feel guilty if they do. As I stated before, Maa is about cause and effects and doing things in the now, which means being spiritual does not mean you are supposed to be a pathetic idiot and let some scumbag do you in. I apologize for the harshness in words, but it is the only way to shock your *sahu* and rid yourself of this flawed thinking that you have to "turn the other cheek." Maa is justice and justice means doing what's right, right now. Maa levels the playing field and when you have someone who is cheating by bullying, victimizing, or harming others just to get ahead. You have the right to do what is necessary to protect and maintain the Maa. But, if you are stuck on "Vengeance being the Lord," you can do this simple Justice Charm asking for help from Hruaakhuti or Osar.

To perform this charm, take a penny to represent the individual and put it in your left hand head side down (tail side up). With your right hand take a purple painted rock or natural brown rock found in nature, and place it on top of the penny, while saying, "Bring (so and so) the same heartache and pain, they gave to others." If you want to use a candle, simply put the penny head side down in a safe dish or candle burner and again with your right hand. Place the brown or purple candle in the burner while making the command. Then light the candle

Once the command has been issued, do not tell anyone about what you did. Discard the materials in nature quietly and do not think about the charm. In fact, it is best to do something completely off the subject to get your mind off of it like watch a movie or play a video game. These actions give your *ba* time to present your petition to the archetypes of justice Hruaakhuti or Osar[19], so that whatever happens to this individual is not your concern. This individual simply brought it upon himself or herself and the emissaries of God served justice.

---

[19] The color brown is not Osar's color but since Osar dwells under the earth and deals with stability a natural colored brown is adequate symbol for him.

101

If a loved one was hurt by the actions of this individual you can perform a Healing Charm the same way, which can be done long distance as well. All you need to do is to simply take a penny to symbolize the loved one (or victim) and put in head side up (tail side down) and place on top of the penny with your right hand a white symbol (rock, candle, etc.). While saying, "Bless and heal (so and so)!" Again, this allows your *ba* to deliver your request to the proper authorities. As before, don't think about how it is going to work. Just trust in the Power of God.

What You Need to Remember to work the Rau #4:
The Time to Act is Now!

I enjoyed reading about religious traditions and practices because it helped me in my quest. For a long time I regretted being raised in a Christian household but as I came to understand that without this background I would not be who I am today. I began to appreciate my upbringing and now I have great respect for those who are in the faith. But what I don't like about Christianity is how sermonizers focus so much on the doom and gloom. I mean everything is about if you don't do this you're going to hell. It almost seems like if catastrophe didn't exist, Christianity would not be successful. I use to wonder why people pile into churches only after a catastrophe strikes. This principle helped me to see that it was because most have made the case that people are going to go to hell because of sins of Adam and Lilith or Adam and Eve, so I believe most people are like why bother. I know this is how I felt when I was a teenager, because it seemed like living like Jesus was just an impossible task and only gets worst.

Thanks to this principle I focus on living for the today and doing what I can today. I live every day to its fullest, so that when I retire my *ab* awareness is free of guilt and worry. If I were to stand before God right now, everything that I have done I would not have any regrets. This is not to say that I am perfect and that all my actions and behavior were ideal, because they surely were not. But, by living each day as if it were my last, it makes me conscientious and responsible for my actions and behavior. I treat everyone I meet respectfully regardless of who they are and not what they have done in the past. When I have wronged someone intentionally I apologize as soon as it is brought to my attention. If I cannot do this, I apologize to that individual's spirit by imagining them and telling them "I apologize." When someone has wronged me, I forgive him or her by telling him or her "It's no problem" or imagining him or her and telling the person's spirit "I forgive him or her." The whole purpose of this practice is clear my conscience, illustrated in the Kamitic tradition as having your *ab* balance a feather. The benefits of following through with this practice are enormous because you will be stress free.

There will be some people that you will find hard to forgive or to apologies to but the beauty is because God's Rau is omniscience, omnipotent and omnipresent. God will already know this and through the Rau you will be able to still overcome these people. The secret is that you cannot allow these individuals to deter you. If you let these individuals deter you, you will find yourself doing something that was not initially planned just to prove a point. There are a lot of people stuck in the past and it is a horrible site to see a man or woman with so much potential on the street, in the shelter, or stuck in a rut because of something someone did whom they have not forgiven. This is why you have to learn to apologize and forgive, so that you can learn to acknowledge and forget in order to live for today.

Code #5: Maa is Love & Love is Exchange

Happiness is anything that gives you self–fulfillment. It is anything that comes from you and in the process makes you and others happy. Happiness and love are often abused because of the profane use of the word love.

Happiness is an essential ingredient in healing. Usually when a person is ill and has a problem recovering from their illness it is because they have lost their happiness and joy. This is partly due to the misinformation that people have about love believing that love comes from things. There is no need to list where this misinformation comes from because we hear it on the radio, see it on television and everywhere. As one who is trying to tap into the Spirit it your responsibility to understand that love comes from within. It is the conscious effort to create and enhance life by harmonizing various influences.

While anyone can paint, it takes a true artist to create a masterpiece. Anyone can boil an egg but a true cook is anyone that can make a delicious meal from scratch. Anyone can bang on a piano or an instrument but it takes a true musician to create music to inspire the world. Anyone can throw words together and make sentences, but only a true master of words can write with meaning and shape the world's consciousness. These individuals that have the ability to do this are successful and remembered throughout time because of their love.

As you learn to tap into the Spirit it is important that you remember the other corollaries because it is this commentary. That has led many of the above individuals to become quite eccentric and elusive. It is a misunderstanding about love that inspires individuals to seek out love from physical things including food, alcohol, drugs and people. True love it must be understood is not abusive, controlling, restrictive, harmful or dangerous. True love is an expression from the Divine. When the Universe was created, God did not do it out of obligation, responsibility, malice or spite. It was created out of love. God enjoyed doing it. When someone creates something to benefit all of humanity, it is done out of love. This is the difference between a person that cooks and an individual that enjoys cooking. True love is an expression of happiness.

One of the reasons why it is important to understand this is because through love we are able to change the world, but don't expect this change to occur overnight. Just like what you know, you didn't learn overnight. We cannot expect others to change instantly or overnight either, because change requires that certain "things" are put in place in order for evolution to occur. The same urges that inspired you to get up in the morning, raise a family, go to work, go to school, better your life, better your situation, etc. has to exist in others in order for them to change as well.

This can be very frustrating at times especially when we see loved ones suffering from the abuse of others, but unless that individual willingly seeks to better him or herself. There is not much can be done. Usually when you hear of an artist taking a hiatus it is for this very reason. They are too attached to the physical realm and find themselves listening and depending upon those in the world. This is why every now and then you will hear a successful artist rant and everyone will think that he or she is crazy. It is because the artists in the beginning learned how to tap into the Spirit for their musical talent and genius, but due to their material success. Begin to depend upon the world for their physical sustenance. Now they find themselves trying to meet the deadlines and top previous successes in order to stay on top.

Fortunately, by understanding that it is the Spirit that gave us what we have and the world can't take it away. You are able to avoid these trappings. Never focus on what it is that you can physically see. Always focus on what you want and stay true to your heart (*ab*).

One of the ways we can use love and happiness to improve our life is by praising what we see in others and wish to desire. For instance, if you the things that you want in life, the things you want in life will manifest them at a much faster rate as well. This is because love is a catalyst.

Love is also a powerful antidote against verbal curses, negative criticism, and the bad intentions of others. Keeping in mind that we are all connected, when a negative thought or idea is issued, it has the ability to wander around in our mind. Then later we find our *sahu* thinking about it constantly, hence given attention to something that we don't want to manifest. To counteract when you hear of someone issuing a negative remark, simply say a prayer or offer a blessing to avert the evil and avoid the obstacle. For instance, if someone says you are stupid. Avert the ill by telling your *sahu* you are a genius. When you hear a person tell a child that they are ugly, stupid and dumb. You simply go back and tell that the child that they are beautiful, intelligent and strong. If you cannot physically do this then issue a blessing their way, because we are all connected the blessing eventually will manifests itself in the child's life either through their own thinking or someone else. If you hear of someone cursing a blessing that you have, stating that you think you are better than others, etc. Avert it by repeating to yourself that "I am blessed and I continue to receive blessings every day." Some other simple remedies that you can repeat to your sahu are: "I look good", "I have perfect health", and so on.

I use this all of the time when I go to the doctor and I am bombarded with all of the advertisements about illnesses suggesting that I try a new medication. I repeat to myself "I am in perfect health" at least enough times to get my *sahu* to think about what I want it to think about. Never forget you are responsible for your own *ab*, so always bless, love and praise yourself daily. Another great way to do this is by the wearing of charms and talismans.

Charms and talismans can be helpful tools in counteracting negative energies and protecting your impressionable *sahu*. They are not complicated to construct and you do not need to go to a specialty store to find these items. All that is needed is something to symbolize what you want. For instance, if you want to be strong, upright and unyielding, a perfect symbol would be a white rock, white bone, or anything you desire to symbolize Osar's strength. If you wanted to symbolize success, then get something such as dollar bill, coin, cowrie shell, whatever and tell your *sahu* that the symbol means you are successful. More will said about this in future chapters.

What You Need to Remember to work the Rau #5:
Love is Supreme

People who have discovered the truth in this principle have noticed that they are most happy when they are sharing their talents with others and don't expect anything in exchange. History in fact reveals that the greatest artists, writers, creators, etc. are those individuals that created something out of nothing because of sheer enjoyment. But as soon as people start trying to do things for money, this is when things go awry. This is when you hear of individuals compromising their ethics, morals and sacrificing their health, wellbeing, relationships, etc. to better their career.

Understand, I am not at all mad at anyone that has done this because I have done it myself several times, but since understanding this principle. I have come to understand that whenever I create something (when done correctly) it is from the *ba*, which means it, was meant to enhance and improve my life and the life of others. Since it comes from the *ba*, it will provide for me whatever it is I need so there is no need for me to compromise my ethics, morals and principles or "sell out".

It is because of a misunderstanding of this code we find people that are materially rich but poor when it comes to their health, relationships, etc. It is because they did not allow their *ba* to show them how to succeed. The way to correct this is by beginning to trust in your *ba* and to follow the maa. When you live for Maa, the Maa pays you back in greater dividends because it is based upon the infiniteness of the KAMTA (spiritual) and not the limitations of the TASETT (physical).

While we're on the subject of love, understand that love is about happiness and it is the secret to good relationships. When you focus your attention on creating happiness you will experience happiness. When a relationship between a husband and wife has turned sour it is because one or both of them are focusing on bad experiences. If one or both of you focus on the good things in the relationship it will increase the good things and may even get rid of the bad in the relationship. This is how new relationships are formed and what makes new relationships exciting. It is the same way new memories are created, which has a strong impact upon the *sahu*.

Code #6: Maa is Order & Not Coincidence

Nothing happens by accidents, chance or coincidence. There is a divine reason for everything whether we are aware of it or not. Since hot cannot exist without cold, fire cannot exist with water, man cannot exist without woman and so on. Success in life is based upon establishing a harmonious relationship with one's opposite. Life for instance is created between the harmonist relationship between the male and female species. A prosperous relationship between a husband and his wife is dependent upon compromise and an even exchange. Success between groups depends upon there being an even exchange of goods and services between the two parties. Success in life is created between the harmonist relationship between the physical and spiritual forces and so on. It is about exchanging and sharing authority.

Maa is about order but order does not necessarily mean neatness. We as human being love for things to make sense. We like to think that there is a logical reason for everything and we try to organize everything in the universe this way to help us to understand the nature of things, but nature doesn't operate this way. There is no good or bad in nature. It is just nature.

Therefore every event and experience you have was created by your thoughts, actions, beliefs, anxieties and expectations. This means that technically speaking there is no such thing as good luck and bad luck. We use the term "good luck" to simply to indicate when something is going our way, and "bad luck" when it is not in our favor.

All the problems that exist in your life are due to there being an imbalance usually from having the wrong beliefs, ideas and thoughts on how to achieve a goal. No one has the ability to make you happy. If you are unhappy it is because you gave your authority to another to subdue you and make you feel powerless. This does not mean that all of the problems that you have in your life are your fault, but it is important to understand that your conscious or habitual response to the events that occur in your life is what contributed to your present situation. When it is accepted that we are the co-creators of our life experience and who or what we choose to share our authority with is what enhances or depletes our life. We will have a better chance of creating the life that we want and increasing our good luck.

What You Need to Remember to work the Rau #6: There is a Reason for Everything

Knowing that nothing happens by accident, chance or coincidence except for that which you give authority to means, what you give authority to is what either empowers or weakens you. This was a very hard lesson for me to learn when my body became ill because raised in the West. I like so many people had the strong desire to want to understand a thing because the more I understand it. The more I believe that I could control it or have power over it. The problem I found out with this approach is that the more I tried to understand the illness. The more I engaged my *sahu* and prevented my *ba* from working on a solution. I noticed that every time I went to the doctor there were all sorts of literature and images of about a particular illness, which made me want to know more. The more I focused by thinking about what I remembered I wanted to know more about it, which made my condition, worsen. It wasn't until it dawned on me to stop contemplating on illness and focus on healthiness and wellbeing that my overall health began to improve. My health improved because I stopped giving authority and power to the illness.

Now, when I say I stopped giving the illness power. I mean I stopped trying to understand the illness and took a nonchalant attitude towards it. I stopped reading books, magazines, and literature about the illness. I stopped watching programs especially those that show people suffering. I even stopped associating with people that didn't share my interest.

The important point about this principle is that everything that exists is a living being. All illnesses or viruses are living beings as well and they have power. As a matter of fact, the difference between a healthy cell and unhealthy cell is that a healthy cell, like the ones that form a wound, work to heal a scrape or laceration. Whereas as a healthy cell, for some reason does not go along with the others or rebels, like Set. So we have to stop seeing things as being so logical and look at life from a holistic perspective.

Through this code you have the ability to tell everything that exist around you to be the way you prefer it. This does not mean you have the right to force your will upon another like some tyrant. It is your right to decide on what you want and do not want in your life. If you want to be healthy declare to your Self to be healthy. If you want a peaceful home, declare that your home will be peaceful. Whatever you want, declare it and allow your *ba* to show you the way to achieving it.

Code #7: Maa is Propriety & Doing What is Relevant

Many people have problems with this principle because they get so boggled down by their beliefs that they believe that there is only one way to do something or accomplish a goal. We hear religious extremists from every corner of the globe claiming that there is only way, which is ridiculous. If there were only one way, why would God allow any other way to exist? There is always another way to achieve a goal.

Not let me clarify because a lot of people misunderstand and misinterpret this to mean that they have the right to bully others into doing what they want. While on the other hand, there are those who take a submissive role and believe that this means that they are supposed to be dominated and suppressed. And, that is not what I am saying at all.

What this means is that you are trying to achieve an objective there is not one way to do it. For instance, there are a number of ways that you can get money. Usually because of limited beliefs, a lot of people think that there is only a couple of ways, which are go to school, work hard so that you can get a good job or, invest in a life of crime. I'm sorry there is a third option that has presented itself and that is becoming an entertainer (actor/actress, athlete, musician, singer, etc.). The most prosperous individuals in the world are neither of these and many of them weren't born with a silver spoon in their mouth. A substantial number of these riche individuals never even went to school, so why are they rich? It is because they learned how to think outside of the box.

If you keep in mind that the world is what you make it because of your thoughts, actions and beliefs, and that everything is connected. Therefore all of your actions will produce a corresponding result. Everything that you do will lead you to accomplishing your goal. You will either be blessed or cursed and again it is all based upon you approach the matter. It is by facing the obstacles before you as a challenge to improve your spiritual skills that you are able to succeed. If for instance, you have a troublesome youth and you just wish they would obey you and be respectful. The challenge before you lies in understanding that physically you cannot achieve the goal, which means you have to tap into the Spirit.

Now, I will be honest with you. I remember the first time I heard this I thought that it meant that if I just meditated on being successful that I was going to achieve instant success. Later, as my understanding of life changed I thought that it meant that I could get anything that I want, as long as I focused upon it. Both of these were wrong. Then one day needing a job to get some more money, I submitted a number of applications, resumes and cover letters to a number of businesses. Then one day out of the blue, I got a call from my supervisor who wanted to know if I would be interested in another job in the same building I was working in. Of course, I took the opportunity and that's when I learned that I got the job because I focused upon what I wanted and let the Spirit figure out how to help me get it.

Learning how to tap into the Spirit requires that you act in faith that you will get what you want and allowing the Spirit to do the rest. Let the Spirit show you the way to achieve your goal, you simply focus upon what you know that you can do. When it comes to recovering from an illness I know very well how agonizing it is to want to know why you became ill and what you can do to overcome it. But, you must resist. After you have seen a good health physician and have done what you can physically do. You have to tap into the Spirit and let the Spirit do the rest. Focus on being in perfect health. I have found it very beneficial to simply recall your life before you became ill and to live as if it never happened. I did this one time when I hurt my eye. Instead of thinking about the pain, I reminded my *sahu* how as a child I had beautiful brown eyes. In a relatively short time the pain ceased. So let the Spirit figure out how to make your dreams a reality. You just need to concentrate on the dream.

What You Need to Remember to work the Rau #7:
Do Whatever Works

There is no such thing as One Way. If it were it would work for everyone but it doesn't because we are all different people with different backgrounds, affiliation and associations. Simply put if you are trying to do something and it doesn't work you need to find another way of solving the problem. If your aggressive behavior is not solving your relationship problems, you may need to try a passive approach. If you have tried every remedy known to man in remedying an illness and it doesn't work. You may need to try a spiritual route. If you have studied the competition, the financial market and various marketing schemes for improving your business with no avail. Then maybe you need to go within and let your intuition show you how to improve your business. You are not restricted to doing one thing. You can do whatever you want to bring Maa (wholeness) back to the situation. Understand, this does not mean do what makes you happy. It means do whatever to restore peace.

For instance, I remember when my body was deathly ill. I used a number of methods to recover from the illness. I danced, sung, wrote, prayed, watched television, played games, exercised and took up the hobby of cooking. I did all of these activities because I noticed that when my *ab* awareness was extroverted I couldn't help but to focus on when I was going to be healed. When I stopped worrying about when I was going to be healed and let my *ba* take care of that. I noticed my recovery rate increased. In fact, the more I acted as if the illness never occurred and just carried on with my life as usual. I recovered at an exceedingly fast rate. When I thought about and talked about the illness it seemed like that's when things worsen. So, now I live my life by trying to remain whole. By this I mean doing whatever I want as if I were in perfect health and if nothing were wrong.

A Final Note

The heroic path I hope you are beginning to see was not about doing whatever you want. Due to the Kamitic people having a relatively short pantheon, the heroic path developed into a practice with little to no official rules that put one in direct communication with his or her ancestors. As a result, the relationship between the initiate and his or her ancestor was a sort of "go as you feel" practice where an individual simply followed their intuition. Through devotion and by adhering to the above principles, the initiate developed a relationship with their ancestor and thereby acquired insight, which would help the initiate in their daily life. Since the spirits are not fettered by the human body. They can intercede on the descendants behalf provided the initiate observed certain taboos in regards to his or her ancestor. Most of the taboos in regards to the ancestors are usually about ethical and moral behavior or adhering to the principles of Maa, which is why it is very important that you strive to adhere to the Maa and avoid engaging in any types of perversions (substance, sexual, etc.). When you follow the Maa the aakhu will assist you in receiving blessings, wisdom and protection from the Divine.

Chapter 7:
The Kamitic Prayer Room

Just like the Prayer Room in the Church is used to tarry for the spirit. The Kamitic Prayer Room is where you will do your spiritual work and work your faith, which is the fuel of the spiritual realm or KAMTA. Faith, remember is not based upon what you see (or have read for that matter), but upon what you know and to work your faith. You have to work with the netcharu and aakhu and see if it works for yourself. By working with the netcharu (especially on an archetypical level) we get a better understanding of the dynamics occurring within our being and the forces of the universe.

As I stated before the netcharu are archetypical spirits. As an archetype they are models that help us to better understand ourselves because they exist throughout the universe. The best way to interact with them is to see them as autonomous beings as Napoleon Hill, the personal success writer and author of the bestselling book, *Think and Grow Rich*.

Hill for those of you who don't know investigated, researched and experimented with the beliefs and theories of successful men and women of his time, in order to find the secret of success. One of the techniques he discovered which were so strange that at one time publishers removed it from the book out of fear that readers would have thought Hill had lost his mind. This technique was called the *Invisible Counselor Technique*.

The technique was simple and can be outlined in three simple steps. First, Hill states that before retiring he would imagine having spiritual meetings with Aristotle, Plato, Homer, Newton, Burbank, Edison and other people whom he felt were very influential. Second, he said that you have to a definite purpose for meeting with them. Finally, he said that you could call on any of the members of this invisible cabinet to comment on his objective. For instance, if you want to discuss leadership you would talk to Abraham Lincoln. Hill admitted that while the meeting was purely fictional and had only occurred in his imagination. The insight, wisdom and ideas that he acquired through these meetings were so powerful and real, that he realized that this was the source of all of our great ideas.

Hill's *Invisible Counselors* is what Swiss psychiatrist Carl Jung called archetypes, which are autonomous entities that have existed since the beginning of time. Jung tried to quantify these archetypes by stating that they exist in the collective unconscious but technically speaking they are everywhere and we use them all of the time. One of the most popular archetypes is Jesus and those who know how to use him correctly, talk to Jesus when it comes to making decisions or ask them self, "**W**hat **W**ould **J**esus **D**o in this situation?" But before they were called archetypes, Plato called them Form, Jews, Christians and Muslims called them angels and djinns. Pagans called them gods and goddess, while the rest of the world referred to them as spirits. When you compare Hill's findings to the maa aankh we see that the deified ancestors are the netcharu, which means now we know where the Kamitic people got their brilliant ideas.

Getting into the Spirit

Now what Hill didn't know (or maybe he did) is that he was doing is what is called a ritual. Although when most people hear the word ritual, what come to mind are people dancing around drums or some clandestine group chanting a bunch of unpronounceable words. A ritual is basically a ceremony that is done with serious intent repetitiously. People perform rituals all the time. Most of our rituals are used to mark the start of something special like a baby showers, bar mitzvahs, quinceanera, rites of passages, debutante balls, graduations, bachelor parties, weddings ceremonies, anniversaries, wake service, funerals, ribbon cuttings, etc. We all perform rituals all the time and for different purpose, but in order for a ritual to be effective. It has to make a lasting impression on us by entertaining our *sahu* and inspiring our *ab*. If it doesn't, the ritual becomes a dogmatic and lifeless practice just done out of tradition, which is why a lot of traditions are abandoned by the youth.

In order to make an effective ritual it must clearly have a purpose in mind. Ritual must consist of a strong beginning to make when the ritual begins and a strong ending letting you know it is over and giving you a feeling of completeness. An effective ritual must also be very appealing, entertaining and charms your physical senses, which is why the most effective rituals have music (hearing), fragrances (such as flowers, incense, colognes, etc. for smell and sight), and consists of some type of physical gesture, movement or physical involvement. The ritual should be done the same way every time but different from any other mundane activity, so that you feel unique and special.

If you will recall from *Chapter 3: Cosmology of the Soul,* you have to make a strong impression upon the *sahu*. The stronger the impression is on the *sahu* the better your chances are in succeeding in create change in your life, but here's the deal. The reason Hill's *Invisible Counselors* made such a strong impression upon him was because it was strange and unusual practice to him initially. Then, the more he used it and the more he became accustomed to it, the easier it was for him to engage in. The same thing applies for us. The stranger the practice may seem the more effective it may be if you understand the symbolism being used. The other thing is that if you are akin to "strange" things like science fiction and horror movies. You may require more "strange" things to shock your *sahu*. For instance, a small skull used to symbolize the dead may make a more meaningful impression upon an individual fond of romantic comedies that might see it as being a bit macabre, as compared to an individual that enjoys science and horror fiction. This is what needs to be taken into consideration when doing a ritual.

An effective ritual does not necessarily need special ingredients or elements. Before moving ahead, I am reminded of the facts that before the Africans were enslaved. They use to have a lot of rituals but when they arrived in the Americas they had to recreate a lot of rituals some more than others. Here in North America, the Africans had to start almost totally from scratch as best they could by relying upon their memory and depending upon their *ba*. They did this by taking ordinary ingredients that they found in their environment and in nature, and used the as tools to survive slavery. This is why I do not list a whole lot of ingredients and symbols that can be used. I will only mention a few basic symbols and allow you to discover your own by working with your *ba*. When you learn to trust you *ba* it will inspire you to make the necessary adaptation to obtain the desired results. You just have to learn to trust your intuition. This will seem difficult in the beginning but with practice you will learn that any time you receive a sudden revelation, especially one that shocks or jolts you, it is coming from your *ba*. This by the way is also how you know that it is not your *sahu* or your own thinking.

There are some basics that I have found to be helpful when doing a ritual like the ceremonial use of symbols. Since all symbols (including music) are entertaining to our *sahu* – our animalistic spirit. When you enter into trance this is when you impress the ideas upon your *sahu*. Dancing, music, and storytelling are some of the more popular ways of impressing new ideas upon the *sahu*. Some other and very powerful ways used in indigenous cultures is the use of tangible items like candles, herbs, stones, pebbles, icons, etc. For instance, one can take a pebble and name it after a particular problem and then toss it over your back into a running river or stream. The analogy is simple; the problem symbolized by the pebble is seen as not being that big of a problem. By symbolically tossing it over your shoulder into a running river or stream, signifies that the problem is being taken away from you. Thereby creating a new experience and making a way for the *ba* intervene on your behalf. If you do not understand how it works, that's good because the less you know the easier it is to convince your *sahu* to follow your lead. All you need to do is have a general understanding so that you can create positive change.

The Purpose of a Ceremony and Ritual

So before we move on, let me state again so that while you are dancing, burning candles or doing whatever it is you do. The purpose of doing a ritual (all of these abstract, interesting, strange and weird practices) is to create the emotions in order to make a deep impression upon your *sahu*. Why are you trying to make a deep impression upon your *sahu*? It is because the only way our *sahu* remembers (or learns) what we want is by associating it with an emotion. This is how we learned how not to put our hand over an open fire because a strong impression was made upon our *sahu* that if we do it our hand will get burned.

Why do we have to do this or why are rituals important? It is because this is one of the most effective ways to influence our beliefs and tie in what we want with our *ba*. Another effective ritual is done through repetition, which is how habits are formed.

The key to a successful ritual is to keep your *sahu* from obsessing over the problem. Remember, it be Divine design tries to figure out what is going on, but it lacks the unlimited ability to do so. If you don't want to think about an elephant, what pops in your mind is an elephant. It is best simply not to worry about the problem and that way you won't think about it either.

116

How do you know when your ritual is effective? You will see the physical results. Now, let's begin.

Colors and How to Use Them

The basic symbols used in any rituals are colors. Colors have a long historical use within our *sahu* and every time we see them. They reinforce what we already know. This is why we've known since we were children that the color red symbolizes hot, fire and means "to stop." As a spiritual tool, colors can be imagined or used as a tangible object like a candle, piece of cloth, food, etc. To bring money to an individual you could baptize a penny in a person's name and sprinkle green grass on top of the penny. As you can see there are endless applications using the simplest of symbols. Below are the common beliefs about colors along with the appropriate command that can be used in trance to create change.

- Black – is used for repulsing, freedom from evil because it resembles the stillness of KAMTA. It therefore, symbolizes the desire for a miraculous outcome from a grim situation. Commands associated with this color are "Absorb!" and "Release!"
- White – is used for healing, spiritual blessing, purification and self – knowledge. Commands associated with this color are "Balance!" "Bless!" "Purify!" "Heal!" and "Enlighten!"
- Royal Blue – is used to create peace, joy, promote healing and harmony. It is associated with sea. Commands associated with this color are "Expand!" and "Empower!"
- Light Blue – gives a feeling of tranquility, inspiration and devotion. It symbolizes the sky and the command associated with this color is "Inspire!" and "Devote!"
- Green – associated with nature's bounty is used for increasing fertility, prosperity, improving business, and looking for a good job. It corresponds to having a new outlook or a fresh start. Commands associated with this color are "Bless!" "Repeat!" "Refresh!" and "Renew!"
- Yellow – is associated with the rays of the sun is used to symbolize money (gold), attraction, creativity, the intellect, the imagination, harmony and prayer. Commands associated with this color are "Adapt!" "Bend!" "Center!" "Create" and "Chase Away!"

- Red – the color of fire is used for enhancing affection, love, and passion. It also symbolizes radiant health, aggression, power, courage and strength, which all emotions used when we our early ancestors first learned about fire. Commands associated with this color are, "Clear!" "Conquer!" "Defeat!" "Protect!" "Remove!"
- Pink – is used for romance, attraction, gentleness, honor and clean living. The command associated with this color is "Clear" which can be used to remove stubborn emotions of gloom.
- Purple – is used for mastery, power, control and command. It symbolizes the deep redness of blood and is used to banish, chase and drive away anything undesired. The commands associated with this color are "Assist!" "Chase!" "Drive!" "Break!" and "Destroy!"
- Orange – is used for opening the way, change of plans, and prophetic dreams, as it symbolizes the midsummer sun and thus excitement, fun, and vitality. The commands associated with this color are "Attract!" "Direct!" "Draw" "Focus!" and "Open!"
- Brown – the color of the earth and therefore the physical plane. It is used for financial matter and for settling disputes over natural resources, hence court matters. The command for this color is "Balance!" This is why things taken from the earth from an indigenous perspective, are giving special offerings of thanks, like a few coins, tobacco smoke, etc.

Power Symbols

Some more useful symbols that you may want to employ are the Aakhu and Aabit, which are commonly called the Eyes of Ra. The Right Utchat also called the Aakhut is used to symbolize the aggressive power of the life force, the left hemisphere of the brain (factual information, letters, numbers, speech, etc.) and all things masculine. And, the Left Utchat called the Aabit symbolizes passive power of the life force, the right hemisphere of the brain (imagination, intuition, symbols, abstract ideas, etc.) and all things feminine in nature. To create a visual trigger go into trance and tell yourself that when you see the Right Utchat or Aakhut it corresponds to the normal, or Beta state of awareness and aggressive power.

Aakhu - The Right Utchat (Eye of Hru):
The Eye of the Sun (Power)

Then tell yourself when you see the Left Utchat called the Aabit it corresponds to twilight, the Alpha or meditative state of awareness and passive power, which will remind you to go within or into trance to resolve your problems.

Aabit - The Left Utchat (Eye of Djahuti):
Eye of the Moon (Trance)

Since you have impressed these ideas upon your *sahu* while in trance, you can place the Right Utchat up anywhere in your house, dwelling or where it as charm to protect against ill thoughts, verbal slander, gossiping, the evil eye, etc. You simply see it as watching over you and your loved ones similar to the Cuban Tongue and Eye.

There are a number of symbols that can be used but so that we are clear. It must be remembered that generally to change our beliefs we need more information along with a new emotional experience, in order for the new belief or idea to become permanent. Unless the belief is a shocking one-time learned experience like being bitten by dog or a snake. Our new beliefs will not be remembered by our *sahu* and it will clash with our old and more powerful beliefs and memories, based upon past experience of being unsuccessful, ill, poverty-stricken, etc., thus convincing us that we will not be able to accomplish our new goals. To create a new experience and change our beliefs, one effective way is to perform rituals like the guardian spirit technique explained below.

Guardian Spirit Technique

There are several ways to work with the netcharu and aakhu, and although it is common in many Afro-Diaspora traditions for practitioners to enter into a state of trance and allow another entity (usually an aakhu) to temporarily replace their conscious awareness. Thus rendering the devotee (also called the spiritual horse) completely unaware of his or her actions, while the possessing spirit performs spiritual healings and give counsel to others through the medium. This is not the case for this practice, which focuses upon entering into a state of trance in order to use the spirit's abilities to create change. It is a type of partnership as was the case for Hru and Osar. For instance, the guardian spirit or spirit guide is called upon to assist in creating change. Through the partnership between the living and the (physically) dead, the spirit offers guidance to the living on how to achieve his or her goal based upon its ability to see beyond the physical limitations. The living and the dead are basically cooperating together to achieve the same goal. This is why it is important to treat your spirits as you would treat your family and friends, because they are your spiritual helpers.

This practice is based upon the hunting and gathering societies dependencies upon the land, when human beings use to live close to the earth and saw it as being sacred, instead of looking at the land and seeing it as a commodity. Understanding that the netcharu have the ability to influence nature means that omens and prophetic signs can come through anything like an animal, falling leaves of a tree, the blowing wind, gentle rain, passing thunderstorm, etc. and, because a peoples' culture is usually tied to the land. It is also possible to communicate with others outside of your culture, which is why this tradition could best described as animism in practice.

This is why it is so very important to live your life according to Maa because one must learn to live in harmony with everything. By doing so, it allows you to achieve any objective through the assistance of others. For instance, by working with certain spirits it can be learned that some plants can be used for spiritual protection without having any foreknowledge of plant. The same can be said about animals and stones.

The following technique is used to work with your aakhu and netcharu. It is inspired by a conversation I once had with Papa who was constantly instructing me to trust my intuition. Since, we already to some extent communicate with spirits on a subtle level (rather we are aware of it or not). We hear their thoughts when we are daydreaming, having lucid dreams, through prayer, contemplation (meditation), hunches or gut feelings, and various other ways. The problem is that for most of us, no one was around to tell us that we were communicating with spirits, so we were encouraged to ignore it. Here we will make direct communication with our spirits.

To begin since, this path is inspired by our aakhu and works primarily with the mind, it doesn't require a lot. Most of the spiritual work can be done using a few simple supplies and basic ingredients found around your house. This way you don't have to worry about other people's energy (negative thoughts) interfering with your aim. It is however preferred that you when doing a ritual you wear white clothing and use this outfit only for this purpose.

1. To begin start the ritual the same way you opened communication to your spirits, by knocking three times (ringing a bell, shaking maracas, etc.) to signal you are entering KAMTA.
2. Say the Lord's Prayer. (For my explanation on why to say this particular prayer see Chapter 5.)
3. Light a candle based upon your objective (see Colors above). If you want healing light a white candle. I first light the wick, and then I light the base if doing constructive work[20] and place the candle in front of the spirit.
4. Proceed to tell the spirit what you are having a problem with, what it is that I want or will need their assistance with. It is important that you are clear about this and you have clear and concise objective in mind, because KAMTA is dark and if you enter into it without any objective. You are bound to spend your time just wandering around aimlessly as if you are doing a mindfulness meditation.
5. You must make maa aankh, that is "swear an oath to live truth" according to the netcharu, which will be explained below. Every

---

[20] If I am trying to rid myself of something, I bite or break the based and light it first and then then wick.

netcharu has a certain amount of taboos that you must follow in order to attract and keep their energy with you. If you wanted to create a romantic mood you wouldn't burn rose incense, pink candles, and then played some hardcore rap, rock or reggaeton would you? It would destroy the mood. Well, the same applies with working with the netcharu, the netcharu (being a spirit) can set the mood but usually it is our thinking (especially our mouth) that messes things up. By making an oath, we are declaring our willingness to work towards the goal from the physical realm. The spirits can't do it all by themselves.

6. Once you are finished close the ceremony by simply saying "Thank you" and leave you concern with the spirit while allowing the candle to safely burn out. Don't think about the outcome. Don't think about what you should have told them. Do something completely different to take your mind off of the subject.

7. When you see signs that your request has been answered. Give the spirit an offering for their assistance. This can be as simple as a white candle, a shot of rum, some candy, some money, some smoke from a cigar, some fruit, whatever to show your gratification.

As you can see, you this practice is about working with your spirits via a partnership, the same way you would in the physical world. The spirits get what they want when you get what you want, so never pay the spirit if your request was not answered. If you don't get what you want then you don't pay and vice versa, which means if you promised some flowers for a request. If the request was answered then honor your promise and pay the spirit their flowers.

Now, if you have worked with your *ba* and have been doing so throughout this discourse you will know that your *ba* will not lead you astray nor will it ask of you to do something that you are not comfortable with or will put your life in danger. Well, the same applies to working with the netcharu and your aakhu, because they work with your *ba*. If you have a problem with alcoholic beverages, your aakhu and netcharu aren't going to ask you this for an offering. They want to see you succeed. Only an aapepu would selfishly do something that is this malicious, so you have to use commonsense, which is why you were instructed to work with your *ba* in Chapter 3.

If you are unsure of a response, you can always test the answer, because your aakhu and netcharu working with your *ba* will understand your natural skepticism. They know that we are naturally skeptic (especially in these days) and the only way to overcome this is by working with them, which increases your faith. So test your responses but do not disrespect your spirits by testing them for financial reasons. This is a spiritual tool and if you use it incorrectly they will abandon you to teach you a very painful and valuable lesson. So, respect your spirits and treat them right and they will do the same for you.

This technique can be done for anything. It can be used to assist you, as well as others, but it can't be overstated that the spirits can't do everything. If you want to lose weight, you can't just make a petition to the spirits and not make a commitment to watch what you eat, exercise or anything. If you want to improve your grades in school, you can't just ask for help but not study for exams or get help in learning a concept that you do not understand. The keys to working this technique are that you have to make a commitment to do your part and allow the spirits to do their part.

Then second, you have to talk to them like you would a friend. Now, when you talk to the spirit, I mean talk to them. The same way you talk to your friends is the same way you should talk to your spirits. Of course be respectful, the same way you wouldn't disrespect your friends you should treat your spirits the same manner. I have to be clear about this because I have heard people say "Oh I would never cuss in front of my spirits," but they cuss in front of their friends. Well, if that is what works for you I say, "Amen" but that doesn't work for everyone and it certainly didn't work for me. When I approach my spirits from a holier than thou perspective, it doesn't move them. In fact, I get a sense that they think I am being *booshie* (or bourgeoisie) and not real. When I get down and out and I don't care, that's when I get a response.

To get a better understand how to work with the netcharu, provided below is a listing of their attributes, the appropriate legends that I have used to help me to understand them; along with information on how to make maa aankh pertaining to the spirit. Since there are not many Kamitic legends about the netcharu that have survived, I am including the stories Papa told me, as well as legends that I have I heard from other sources. Please note that most of the legends of the orisha may not be authentic tales from Yoruba and maybe Papa's rendering of the original tale or how to legend was told to him in Cuba.

Osar, Guardian of Peace

Osar is the king of the netchuru and lord of the Underworld As Lord of the Underworld, he represents the one that governs and is over the entire unknown and mysteries of the universe. Mystically speaking, Osar is the one that stands at the edge of the universe and totally oblivion, thus giving him the uncanny ability to see the purpose of everything. This is how he first learned of the Maa and was able to teach the Kamitic people about it.

Osar, manifests himself as benevolence, patience, wisdom, peace and power. He is an idealist that loves order, peace and cleanliness. He teaches people how to peacefully work together for a common accord by helping people to see the importance of everything. He is a wise and loving ruler that teaches people to live an ethical and moral life by adhering to the Maa. All Osarian archetypes are seen as the high chief, the king of kings, the lord of lords, and the first to build, create or establish something to benefit all of humanity. In the case of Osar, he is seen as the founder of the Kamitic civilization and so on. There are other Kamitic legends that speak about how Osar is the founder of civilization as well, but to discuss this would take us beyond the scope of this book. There are numerous stories that Papa told me about all of the divinities that helped me to better understand and see them in my life. The one story in particular he told me that helped me to understand Osar was about the Yoruba creator story and the orisha Obatala.

Obatala, Yoruba Orisha of Creation

Legend goes that in the beginning there was only the sky above ruled by Olorun, the Lord of Heaven, and nothing but water below, ruled by Olokun. One day Obatala wanted to create some land for all of the people to live. So he went to Olorun who granted him permission and then he went to Orunmila for advice to inform him upon what he needed to do. Orunmila, the wise orisha of prophecy to Obatala that he would need a gold chain long enough to reach below, a snail shell full of sand, a white hen, black cat and a palm nut. All of the orishas helped Obatala gather up the gold so that he could create the golden chain. When he had everything

124

assembled, Obatala hung the chain from the corner of the sky and climbed below.

When he reached the end of the chain, seeing that there was some distance from him to go, Orunmila told him from above to pour the sand from the snail shell out and then release the white hen. Following Orumila's guidance Obatala pour the sand out and released the hen, which scratched and spread the sand around all about the watery abyss. Everywhere the sand fell, dry land formed and finally valleys and hills were created.

Obatala then dropped from the chain and named that place Ife, the capital of the Yoruba kingdom. Then he dug a hole and planted a palm nut, which instantly grew into a palm tree and relinquished more palm nuts to the ground, and these seeds instantly grew as well, and the process continued until all of the land was full.

Obatala surveying the dry land with the black cat accompanying him on his side, became bored be alone so he decided to create others like him. So he dug a hole from the clay he found in the ground and molded figures like him. Again he became bored of the process, so he decided to take and break from creation and make palm wine from a nearby palm tree. Drinking bowl after bowl, he became drunk as he continued to make figures from the clay. When he finally finished, he asked Olorun to breathe life into his creations. When Olorun looked down and saw the figures that Obatala had created he noticed that there were some perfect figures and a number of them that had imperfections, because they were created when he was drunk. Obatala having no idea what he had done, Olorun scolded him. The next day when Obatala realized that some of his creations were deformed because of his excessive drinking, he vowed never to drink alcohol ever again. And, since that time all deformed children including albinos were seen as his special children.

It is from this story when compared with the Story of Osar I came to understand that when we are tasked to complete a very important project, we must at all times remain sober. It is our responsibility and if we fail we will always be reminded of it.

Another thing that is central to this archetype is the color white and as the father of civilization, creation, etc. is the foundation. This is why Osar is associated with foundations, infrastructures, mountains, the underground (hence the underworld), bones (especially the spinal column hence the djet also called a column), etc. All of these are puns on Osar's strength, which require ones to be sober.

Working With Osar

Most work with Osar consists of you learning how to resists the temptation to fight, engage in violent acts and over consumer substances. Osar wants you to have a cool head. He wants you to be strong, moral, ethical, and upstanding and resist the temptation of the lower lands. He wants you to bite your tongue and keep the peace. He assists in helping you to obtain peace of mind, general good health, control of emotions, success in academic affairs, material wealth, developing patience and acquiring wisdom. When working with him regarding any of these situations you must write a list of the scenarios that will cause you to lose your peace, your cool, blow your temper, etc. regarding the situation you are working on. Simply ask Osar to assist you in achieving your goal while making a commitment not to lose your cool.

Oset, Guardian of Change

Oset is the matriarchal head, the symbol of motherhood, the protector of families and pregnancies. She is the bringer of prosperity for those who petition her for financial relief and the ruler of the home. She is netchar that gives us exactly what we need. As the queen–mother of Kamit, Oset is the establisher of rules (not the creator of rules). It is not that she creates rules. She just likes things to be done a certain way. When I think back upon my childhood of how my mother and grandmother were with my brothers, cousins and I. It helped me to see that Oset doesn't raise her children to be her friends. She is all about teaching her children the necessary skills (ethical, social, etc.) they need to do in order to survive. Like any good mother she will do whatever she has to do (even if it requires putting her life in danger) to protect her children, as seen in the *Story of Ra and Oset* to obtain Ra's secret. In this sense, she is syncretized with the Virgin Mary. Her motherly meekness turned violently strong when her loved ones are in danger syncretized her with the orisha Yemaya, the Mother of the Sea. Oset is a beautiful and lovely mother, but she can hold a grudge for a long time.

One thing I have found out about Oset from observing my mother, grandmother and mothers in general is that when they want something done, if you do not get up and do it when they want it. They will find a way to make it happen even if it means putting themselves in harm's way. It is from this perspective it is easy to see that Oset is the mother of all revolutions. When you see children fighting in wars, this is Oset in a desperate situation fighting for survival. Oset is strong very strong and it is male chauvinism that has made her appear to be weak, but as Papa once told me about her Yoruba counterpart Yemaya.

"Yemaya is stronger than Chango and Oggun because she can easily put out their fires with her waves."

There's one story I remember my mother told me about my grandmother that helped me to see this. My grandfather was a brick mason and like most construction work in Michigan during the middle of the 20th century, it was seasonal. Now, this was before my grandfather had joined the church. Anyway, as the story goes my grandfather got into an argument with my grandmother. My grandfather became so angry that he threw a plate down on the kitchen floor. My grandmother sitting in the room with the children watching him was apparently not moved by his anger. She told him in a stern voice, "You are going to pick up every piece of that broken plate. " I think this made my grandfather even more upset because she was not frightened by his manly display of anger. She then told the children, "Children, be careful when walking around that glass," which must have angered him even more, so he stormed out of the house and slammed the door behind him. My Mom told me that the broken glass stayed in the floor for hours. She said that she thought the whole argument was stupid and that she wanted to pick up the plate by my grandmother insisted that she didn't. It was truly a battle of the wills. Some hours later, my grandfather came into the house and without saying much. He swept the floor and picked up the broken pieces of the plate.

Why did my grandfather pick up the broken plate? Did my grandfather fear my grandmother? Why didn't she allow my mother to pick up the pieces of broken plate? I don't actually know the answers why because I was told this story I believe after my grandparents' passing. I believe the reason my grandmother didn't pick up the pieces of the plate and insisted that children didn't. Was to teach them all a lesson, which was that no one who claims to love you has the right to talk to you and treat you badly, regardless of how bad they feel. I believe my grandfather realizing his wrongdoing and seeing how he acted in front of his children made him feel even worse. Whatever the case, it was the only time and the last time my grandfather and grandmother had an argument like that ever again according to my mom their eldest child.

When I think about this story, it reminds me of how the women of Liberia organized in 2003 to bring an end to the civil war that was occurring in that country. It is said that the women who were tired of the fighting staged a peaceful and nonviolent protest, which included a sex strike and threats of curse[21]. Along with brokering a peace deal, it brought about the election of the first African female president Ellen Johnson Sirleaf.

There are a lot of women who have birthed revolution, which is why you can't have a real revolution without women. Some of the most memorable women that come to mind who are inspired revolution are Queen Nzingah and Mvita Kimpa of the Kongo (the One Who Fights Against the System – the Porugese Rule), Granny Nanny of Jamaica, Mariana Grajales Coello of Cuba (mother of Antonio Maceo Grajales also known as the Bronze Titan, Yaa Asantewaa of the Ashanti, and many others including Joan of Arc. This is why Papa told me that Oset is a warrior and it is her ability to "see (psychically)" and strength that made her treasured in most indigenous societies. This is why Oset is honored as a queen mother but seen as warrior.

Oset is crafty, as you read in the *Story of Ra and Oset*, she can devise of ways to get whatever she wants. Interesting, the Yoruba tell a similar story of how Yemaya tricks Orunmila the orisha of divination into tricking him into teaching her divination. These are all clear signs of how there is nothing that can stop her from achieving what she wants because she has a strong will, but she is also loyal. Meaning if you do not cross her and take care of her, she will clearly go all out to do what she must for you.

Working with Oset

Oset governs pregnancy, motherhood, she is the symbol of motherhood, protect of children, family health and wealth. I have found that working with her usually centers on something that trouble us and we regret. This

---

[21] For more information see the documentary *Pray the Devil Back to Hell.*

can be something that we have seen in the past that we regret and don't want to repeat; or something that might happen, which we will later regret. Whatever the case, it has to do with regret. This regret could come from something we did, said or learned when we were younger or some other stage in our life. As a result, it (Set) is causing problems in our life right now.

To work with Oset, write a list of everything negative you have learned, said or experienced pertaining to your objective that she governs. If you cannot remember the whole situation don't worry about it. Just write down what you can remember and let Oset help you with the rest. Now, because a lot of times you may not know recall what you have done wrong or what wrong was done to you. You let Oset assist you in this matter by lighting a white candle. Next, tell Oset, "Whatever has been done in the past is in the past. I completely forgive it Oset. "This should be repeated several times at least for a minute or longer if possible.

The objective of this ritual is not to forget what was done but to forgive so that you can grow from the experience instead of allowing the stress from the regret to hold you down. You should after repeating this feel better and the stress from the regret wash away. When you begin to see signs of improvement from Oset, thank her by light a blue candle to Oset and ask her assistance in the matter. Continue to do the above steps until you see a change. When you do a see sign of change make an offering giving her thanks.

I have found that a lot of time when we suffer from regret it is due to the criticism of those whom we respect. This could come inadvertently from our families and friends who are sharing with us their opinion, or it could come from some individual of authority like a doctor, teacher, etc. who tells us based upon his or her "professional" opinion that we are going to fail, can't succeed, won't recover, etc. As a result, even though we may try to achieve our goals, these doubting ideas and thoughts linger around in the back of our mind. This makes us doubt our abilities and causes our faith to waver, because we now wonder if either something "bad" is going to happen or that something is wrong. The above ritual can also be used in washing away these unproductive ideas and thoughts. It is usually a good idea to forgive and accept that a lot of times these individuals didn't know anything about the nature of the spirit.

It is important that you do not criticize, because criticism is like being punched in stomach, which explains why when we hear censure, we cringe and brace ourselves. Remember, Oset is a mother and she wants to nourish her children. A good mother doesn't tear down their child and tell them that they can't accomplish anything. On the flipside a good mother doesn't give into their child's temper tantrums and tell them whatever they want to hear. A good mother tells their child what they need in order for them to survive and function in society. So, Oset wants us to know that if you really care about the situation that you came to her about, you will try your best to be as gentle as you can but honest. This means that if you have to criticize someone or something. Try to break the news to them as gentle as you can but be honest. This can be accomplished by first complimenting them, while suggesting that they try another approach, and then ending with a compliment.

Hru, Guardian of Justice and True Heir to the Throne

Hru is the guardian of justice and the true heir to the throne of Osar. Hru is netchar that ensures that we don't get walk over and used as a doormat. If your boss is barking orders and you walk out on the job thinking you're going to get him or her back, but without having another job prepared to go to. You may have won the battle but you're about to lose the war, because now you don't have any money and may have to go back and ask for that job back or your ex-boss' assistance. Now you have as the saying goes egg on your face.

Hru is a strategist. He is not the best strategic planner, Djahuti is the best, but he is good. He is a fast and creative thinker who eclipses his fear with courage, which makes him a powerful force for justice. Unfortunately, his lack of wisdom makes him easy prey for Set to manipulate and take advantage of. There are numerous stories of how Hru and Set fought and most of them all have to do with Hru's ego, excessive pride and rashness, which is why he is easily identified with the strong of the bible Sampson and King David.

Common amongst most heroic archetypes is the loss of sight. When Set got close enough to Hru he was able to gouge out the young warrior's eyes. We find a similar analogy in the story of the biblical Sampson who lost of his strength, and sacrificed his sight because of his ego, pride. To right the wrong, a classic example of a true hero is self-sacrifice to remove the guilt and shame. There were several stories I heard of from Yoruba practitioners about Chango, which all seems to correspond to his military prowess and use or misuse of power.

Chango Kills His Family

One story claims that one day Chango the son of Obatala who had married Oya, Oshun and Oba, had acquired a powerful charm from his father that allowed him to vanquish his enemies. Chango ate most of the sacred medicine and given the rest of the sacred medicine to Oya to hide, but when he turned around. She consumed the rest of the medicine. The next morning when he saw his wives and children, he opened his mouth to greet them but the horrific fire that exited his mouth consumed them all. Regretting what he had done, Chango took his life but soon after became an orisha.

There are a number of stories that relate to Hru. The one Christian story that relates to Hru is the story of David and Bathsheba.

The Story of David and Bathsheba

According to 2 Samuel 11:1 says: King David has sent Joab out with the entire Israeli army to destroy the Ammonites and besieged Rabbah, while he remained in Jerusalem. One evening David is said to have gotten up from his bed and walked around on the roof of the palace. From the roof he saw a beautiful woman bathing so he sent someone to find out who she was. When his servants returned back, they told him that the woman was Bathsheba, the daughter of Eliam and wife of Uriah. Without hesitation, David ordered his messengers to get her and have her come to him. When she did following the king's orders she lay with him and went back home, but became pregnant.

To hide his sin of adultery, David suggested to Bathsheba's husband Uriah to return home and lay with his wife, so that it would seem that he conceived the child. But Uriah refused to follow David's request because he felt it dishonorable to abandon his fellow soldiers in the midst of battle. So, after numerous failed attempts David sent word to his head general Joab to arrange for Uriah to be on the front line where he would be one of the first to die in battle.

When David realizes that he has committed adultery and murdered to cover up his sin. He repents to the Lord asking for total forgiveness and for his heart to be purged of all the guilt, shame and sin that he has committed.

Another Yoruba story that reminded me about the power of Hru is the story of Chango and his transformation.

The King is Not Dead

In another legend it was said that Chango was a very tyrannical warrior king but when war came to an end. For his own amusement he formulated a plan to get his two closest friends and the generals of his army to fight each other to the death. The men pleaded to Chango not to force their hand but Chango would not listen and even went so far that he threatened to do harm to the two men's families. Finally, when the men heeded their king's order and killed each other in battle. When Chango finally came down off his power high and saw how he had abused his authority. A great grief had overcome him as he realized how he had killed his best friends, made their wives widowers, their families fatherless and his armies weak because of the loss of their generals. Shamed by his arrogance, Chango fled from the village and hung himself in a tree. When his wife Oya found the dead king's body, showing him no mercy, elevated the king's spirit.

As news of the dead warriors spread throughout the land, Chango's enemies upon hearing the death of the king decided to take advantage of loss and decimate Chango's kingdom. But the remainder of Chango's army managed to find their dead king's body and when they found the lifeless body. Partially in denial and to spread fear amongst Chango's enemies, to take advantage of his powerful reputation, they strategically shouted "*Oba ka so! Oba ko so!* (The King is not dead! The King is not dead!)", to prevent their fragile kingdom from being overrun. By shouting this announcement, Chango's enemies were forced to reconsider their plans, and this declaration later became the battle cry for them to defeat and maintain their kingdom.

Now I have heard people ask when they read about Chango and Sampson, if this means that suicide is okay in traditional African thinking. This is not to be taken literally as Papa once told me about being

132

superstitious. What Hru, Chango Sampson, David the entire heroes and heroines do when they take their life is a symbol of self – sacrifice. Self-sacrificing is when an individual sacrifices his or her desires for the sake and wellbeing of others, which is why they are considered heroes or martyrs. This is completely different from an individual that committed a heinous act, got caught and rather than face the consequences of their actions they end their life. For instance, the most memorable hero of our time at present is Dr. Martin L. King Jr., who was aware of the threats to his life but continue to fight for what he believed.

Working with Hru

Hru is about the correct use of power. He wears the double crown to remind him at all time to keep a cool and wise head, thus guided by Osar. Hru makes sure that no abuses or misuses us and reminds us that our *ab* is free. We have the right to do whatever it is that we want, but that doesn't mean we should do whatever we want. The freedom that we have requires that we be responsible for our actions and behaviors. This means we always need to consider the consequences of our actions and behaviors, because we are the only one's responsible for our *ab*.

It is important to understand that no one can take your *ab* (your soul or your power)! The only way an individual takes your power, your *ab* is if you let them and allow that individual to have it. When you feel that someone or some "thing" is tugging at your *ab*. You have to make a firm decision that they cannot have it and fight for it. And, here's where Hru come in, to help you fight for what is rightfully yours.
To work with Hru, write out what you want. Tell him how tired you are of being abused and misused. Tell him how you are tired of being on end and getting walked over. Tell him how tired you are of having your neck stepped on and how you want to stand up and get the monkey off your back. Take something small like a pebble, a penny, etc. to symbolize your objective. Then light a red candle and stand it up on your objective. Make a commitment to fight with all of your might and ask Hru to assist you. Continue to do the above steps until you see a change. When you see signs that your situation is improving, thank Hru by giving him an offering.

Djahuti, Guardian of Divination

As I have mentioned earlier, the purpose of listing the Yoruba legends within these pages is because these are the stories that Papa told me, which helped me to better understand the energies within and around us, as well as to draw comparisons with them in other traditions. Papa was the one that encouraged me to syncretize, understanding that you cannot restrict the spirit to a box. That being said, I am aware that some of these tales are considered New World creations and in this light, (by some purists) are not considered to be authentic, because they do not come directly from Africa. I mean no disrespect, but if it were meant for any traditional religion to be practiced the way it was in the Old World, it would have been done so. As Papa once told me when I asked why Santeros mask the face of the orishas and continue to syncretize them the saints and other archetypes in other traditions even though it is not necessary. The reason he explained was because we still live in a hostile environment where syncretism is necessary. While it is true that slavery is officially over and organized religions do not persecute people because they have different beliefs (Right?), it is those who are closest to us that persecute us now because of cultural beliefs. The negative portrayal of anything African still haunts people. Although it might sound great to shock someone with the truth by not masking cultural beliefs and practices, in reality there's a two-edge sword and you'll find yourself branded as the strange one in your family. There's a saying, "You can attract more flies with honey then you can with vinegar," meaning syncretism is our honey.

He explained to me that syncretism is how black people throughout the Caribbean, North and South America survived slavery. He went on to say that the Yoruba religion as it is practiced in Africa would not have survived here in the New World, because the Africans were living in a totally new environment. Along with slavery and racism, they had to adapt to a society that created and developed an entire system meant to subdue and make all people of color feel inferior in every way.

These courageous Africans had to alter their beloved religious orders just to survive and then hundreds of years later, people talk about what is not authentic. Clearly, the claim that something is less or more authentic is a system of control meant to bastardize the experiences of others. It is the same argument that Catholics have with Protestants; Jews have with Christians and Christians with Muslims and so on. When we consider the fact that those traditions that desperately tried to hang on to the old ways without adapting, we can read a short paragraph about them in history books. This argument about authenticity we see is really silly. If the tradition confers the Maa, meaning simply that it works, that should be authentic enough.

The Legend of Orunmila

One of the stories that Papa told me that helped me to understand this was the story of Orunmila the Yoruba orisha of divination. According to legend, Oggun was in love with his mother Yemmu and had concocted a plan to make ravage love with her when his father Obatala was away. When Obatala left, Oggun fed the divine rooster Osun, Ellegua's food so that he would overeat and fall asleep. Then he would kick Ellegua out of the house to go play so he wouldn't see him shamefully possessed Yemmu sexually. Then before Obatala would return Oggun would leave. Apparently after this had gone on for a quite while Obatala noticed that Ellegua had lost a great deal of weight. When he inquired Ellegua as to what was going on and why he was losing so much weight. Ellegua told Obatala, "When you're away. Oggun feeds my food to Osun, so that he can fall asleep. Then he orders me to go play outside, while he makes love to Mother."

Obatala's eyes filled with tears but he wanted to see if there was any truth to what Ellegua was telling, so he packed his bags and pretended like he was going on a trip. When he left, as before Oggun came into the house, fed Osun Ellegua's food and forced Ellegua to go play outside, while he ravaged his mother. When Obatala returned, he found as Ellegua had told him, Osun sleep while he was locked outside, so he busted into the house and there he found Oggun and Yemmu in bed naked. Full of shock and shame, Oggun covered himself but when Obatala raised his hand to curse him. Oggun pleaded to his father not to curse him but to allow him to curse himself. Obatala agreeing, Oggun declared that he would toil every day and night without rest, and that he would give human beings his secret of how to forge iron. With that Obatala approved of his curse and commanded that Oggun leave and never return.

Turning his gaze upon Yemmu, he told her that he could not curse her because she was his half. Instead he told her that the next male child that she would have he would kill. A year later, Yemmu gave birth to a male child an incarnation of Ifa (the Wisdom of God), Music and

Wisdom whom she named Orunmila, but Obatala true to his word took the child and buried him at the foot of Iroko, the goddess of all trees. Believing that the child was dead, Obatala left but the Iroko tree had pushed the head of infant above ground and miraculously was kept alive.

A year later Yemmu became pregnant again and gave birth to another male child, Chango but Chango was so beautiful that Obatala couldn't bring himself to kill him. The child was so beautiful that he wsa the only thing that brought him joy, which he lost ever since Oggun's banishment and Yemmu's punishment. So, he ordered his eldest daughter Dada to raise him and keep him away from Yemmu, but asked her to bring Chango to visit with him.

Meanwhile, Ellegua found Orunmila's head above ground by the Iroko tree and had returned there routinely to give him food. Ellegua had promised that one day he would tell Obatala about him so that he could release him from his bondage, but Orunmila told Ellegua that he was not in any rush. That the Iroko tree had provided for him everything that he needed, but Ellegua was not convinced. So a number of years later, Ellegua told Obatala that Orunmila lived because the Iroko tree kept him alive. When Obatala demanded to be taken to him, Ellegua took Obatala to the tree where the face of Orunmila rested above ground.

Obatala full of joy commanded that the earth open up and he picked up the scrawny, naked little boy up and hugged him with all of his might, while asking him to forgive him. But, Orunmila exclaimed "You have nothing to apologize for Father. Whatever it is you do, you do for a reason and this everyone must accept as truth."

Obatala covering Orunmila with his robe told issued that they should go home, but Orunmila refused saying that "The Iroko tree is my home because she is the only Mother I have ever known."

Obatala raised his hand and transformed the Iroko tree to a tray telling Orunmila, "Now everywhere you go, you can carry Iroko with you."

As time went by, Orunmila had become a pretty good diviner but the Almighty God, Olodumare, had given Chango his boon the art of divination and prophecy. Chango however was not all that fond of it his talent, he preferred music. So one day he decided to trade it for

136

Orunmila's boon of Music. The two agreed and made the exchange, and that's how Orunmila became the orisha of divination and wisdom.

Working with Djahuti

I remember when Papa first told me this story, Orunmila's exclamation to Obatala that he didn't have to apologize to him; because everything he does has a reason helped me to stop wondering why slavery happened. It helped me to accept that sometimes things happen that we are aware of and that we have no control over, but we can't live in the past or be mad. At the same time, he helped me to understand that you have to make adaptations because nothing is static.

I arrived at the above conclusion because the interesting part of the story to me was that Orunmila's body being buried under the ground with his head expose above ground seemed to refer to the allusion of stillness in regards to wisdom. This is the same reason why the ibis, cranes and storks, which stand on one leg, are Djahuti totems. Another interesting thing is that the "dj" in his name also can be found in the name of the white crown of Osar, the Hedjet and the djet, referring to the backbone of Osar. All of these are puns to inner strength, stillness and wisdom. In other words, Djahuti's is all about obtaining outer peace from inner peace, which comes about from ignoring everything that is going on in the outer world. When you ignore what is going on in the outer world and focusing your attention on one thing. You have just introverted your conscious awareness, but with Djahuti it is more in depth.

Working with Djahuti is all about learning how to train and focus your mind on something for a continuous amount of time. In general, the basic technique for accomplishing this is called meditation and involves you focusing your conscious mind on one thing until the desired change occurs within and outside of your being. People all over the world since the first human being learned to meditate have been doing this and have developed numerous ways to make this change occur. Some cultures have created unpronounceable words to be chanted, others have sung, played drums and dance, while others have developed ways of creating this change by simply gazing at image or touching certain objects. Whatever the technique, the basic objective is still the same, to focus on your attention on one thing in order to create a change within and without. This is all meditation is but so many people think it involves you sitting in a lotus position, with fingertips touching and chanting "OM', while this is one technique it is not the only one. So, to divorce us from this idea, I prefer to use the word contemplation instead of meditation, because it reminds me that I am like an ibis staring into the depths of a river watching its prey.

To work with Djahuti, write down the problem on a blank sheet of paper or symbolize the problem with an image. Ask Djahuti to help you to resolve the problem peacefully. Then focus on the desired subject and allow whatever thoughts, ideas and feelings related to the subject to flow through your awareness. When a solution is received simply express your gratitude to Djahuti and implement it into your life. If you want to make an offering, you can offer a glass of water and this is acceptable.

Now, most people contemplate all of the time especially when it comes to planning or studying. The difference here when you work with Djahuti is that when you focus your attention to solve a problem. You will do so expecting a positive result but, while at the same time being nonjudgmental. This means for instance if you want to solve a problem that you focus on the issue and allow all of the thoughts and ideas regarding the issue to pass through your awareness. Since you entered into this mental dialogue with Djahuti expecting to get a something positive solution, you don't cease your meditation until a positive answer appears to you intuitively. It is like thinking that no matter how bad the situation appears, something good is going to come out of it.

Nebhet, Guardian of Beauty and Sensuality

Nebhet is seen as the embodiment of love and sensuality. She represents happiness and joy, and is the energy that makes life worth living. Nebhet is the patron of riches, fertility and marriages, and the netchar that teaches humanity how to love. Nebhet's colors are yellow, gold, pink and green. She loves all shiny things like jewelry and is fond of perfumes. Her offerings are: oranges, tropical fruits, passion fruit, pumpkins, champagne, and fruity mixed drinks. Her number is five and its multiples like 25.

Most of the identifications we have Nebhet are negative ones because Western society is very chauvinistic. Femininity and sexuality were not well thought of in the West and for several centuries were viewed as sins. When we think of love and sexuality, automatically what comes to mind is the naïve Venus or vengeful Aphrodite of the Greeks or the evil of Lilith (Adams' first wife according to Jewish lore), the deception of Eve over Adam and Delilah over Samson. Many conservative Christian are quick to point to Sodom and Gomorrah as being the result of this energy, and fear that the same fate will soon happen to contemporary man, which has led to the persecution of women that continues to exist today. But Nebhet is a natural energy and like any invisible force. You can't dam it up and suppress it. It has to be allowed to flow, which means you have to learn the correct way to direct it. This is why the Lucumi (Yoruba of Cuba) identification of Nebhet is called Oshun and she is associated with all rivers. Rivers are a perfect analogy of Nebhet because they indicate that just like love and sexual energy is gentle and smooth flowing like fresh water. If dammed, suppressed or not managed carefully. They can become extremely violent and destructive, then after the chaos has been done. The waters return back to being gentle and smooth flowing. Sexual perversion, sexual promiscuity, prostitution (all forms), addictions, etc. are all the destructive sides of Nebhet allegorized in the Kamitic legend as when she was married to Set.

As you can see, when we stop thinking that Set is some impish being running around on hind legs, carrying a pitchfork and see him for being what he truly is, a chaotic and destructive force. We see that Set manifests himself with Nebhet in our actions and behaviors whenever we bully and suppress women suppress feminine energy, abuse sexual energy, misuse substances, etc. Eventually Nebhet will express herself and it may not be pretty. So, since most of us are familiar with Nebhet's destructive side, I will share a couple of stories that will give insight to her more constructive aspects or when she is aligned with Osar. There are two Yoruba legends that I learned that refer to this.

How Oshun Brought Ogun Back to Civilization

Although Oshun is the favorite wife of the orisha Chango, some of her most memorable feats are with Ogun. It is said that there was a time when Obatala banned the Ogun form civilization for some apparent misdeed. So, Ogun not wanting to be bothered by anyone, made his new home deep in the jungle, but he hadn't finished teaching humanity the secret to working iron. It wasn't long afterwards that the community began to decline because of Ogun's absence. So, when the people cried out to Obatala how they much they needed Ogun. Obatala declared that Ogun should be reinstated back to his original station as the chief blacksmith,

139

although he would continue to be banned. Relieved, a search party went out to find him, where it was learned that he was deep in the jungle at the other end of the country. When Ogun heard the news that Obatala had reinstated as chief blacksmith and that he should return. Ogun stubbornly refused comply, citing that he had no reason to return. Finally, after several failed attempts, Oshun had offered to entice Ogun back by using a magical pot of honey. Slowly she spread the glistening sweet substance all over her naked and curvaceous body. Then she went out into the jungle to find Ogun. Ogun's acute sense of smell led him right to Oshun. When he found the beautiful orisha, Oshun seeing that her beauty overwhelmed him, took her honey-dipped finger and gently put it in Ogun's mouth. Ogun unable to resist Oshun's beauty, charm and allure followed Oshun as if he was in a trance and kept trying to embrace her, but each time he advanced. She managed to slip away and have him continue to follow her back to community. When they arrived Obatala told Ogun that he could retreat back to the jungle but he must continue teaching humanity the science of Iron, because without him civilization would come to standstill. Ogun being an obedient orisha complied and this Oshun brought Ogun back to civilization.

How Oshun Made Oggun Settle Down

In another story I learned about Oshun and Ogun also involved the orisha of the sea, Yemaya. In this legend, Onire, an attribute of Ogun was known as being a wild man especially sexually had gained a reputation of having his way with women then leaving. One day Yemaya after hearing of Ogun's sexual prowess had expressed that she wanted to experience Onire's passion, so she ventured out to jungle to find Onire. Sure enough when he found her, Onire had his way with her and as he had done with other women, he left. The beautiful Yemaya upset and distraught by what Onire had done. Fled to Oshun's house to cry upon her sister orisha's shoulder. She told Oshun that she had wanted to marry Onire but that he had abandoned her in the jungle. Oshun appalled with Onire's behavior devised a plan and again once again spread her magical honey over her beautiful and curvaceous body. Then she tied five yellow kerchiefs around her waist and went into the jungle. When Onire encountered the beautiful orisha, Oshun danced before him and as before the two had relations, but this time. Onire mesmerized by Oshun's honey expressed his desire to want to make love with Oshun again, which she replied it would be better if they went to her home.

So Onire followed Oshun to her home, but instead of taking him to her house she went to Yemaya's. When she arrived Onire was led inside and again he engaged in mad sex but, unbeknownst to him. He made love to Yemaya and not Oshun. In a relatively short time, Onire married Yemaya and that's how Oshun made Ogun marry and settle down.

In both of these legends we see that honey is used to symbolize what entices us. It doesn't just represent feminine sexual energy but anything that is used to grab our attention and entice us. This is what love is all about. Love doesn't make you afraid, anxious or worrisome. When you are in love you are happy. You feel like there is nothing in the world that can stop you. When you "fall in love" you don't focus on the things you don't like or all of the things going wrong. You focus on the things of beauty and you talk about your dreams. All of the things that prevent us from experience Nebhet's love, happiness and joy are all of the inhibitions of our *sahu*, which Set rules.

Set rules with anger, despair, fear, guilt, resentment and worry, and this is how he controls Nebhet. To get Nebhet to leave Set and align herself with Osar, if you are having problems finding love, issues with marriage, problems with your finances, etc. Try the following ritual.

Working with Nebhet

Write out a list of all the things that make you angry, feel despair, disgusted, afraid, guilty, resentful and worrisome in regards to your relationship. If working on finances, then make a list in regards to your present financial situation, and so on. For a marriage if possible, it is best that both the husband and wife do this ritual for faster results.

Since whatever our mind is focused on we attract to ourselves due to the Second Code of Maa. After you made your list you need to understand your situation has become worse because this was the energy blocking you, your relationship, your finances, etc. Set had you focused so much on the things that you did not want; it was hard to see what you wanted. A lot of times you will find that you were very critical and cynical. So now, take the list and burn it and flush the ashes down the toilet.

Make a commitment to see the things that you want out of life. Begin by not criticizing in regards to your objective. For instance, if doing this ritual for your marriage. You would not criticize your husband or wife for the things they do, because this will only cause them to most likely do it more, either out of resentment or subconsciously from fear.

Once you make the commitment, now light a yellow candle to Nebhet and ask for her assistance in the matter. Continue to do the above steps until you see a change. When you see signs that your situation is improving, thank Nebhet by giving her an offering.

Npu, Kamitic Guardian of the Crossroads

Have you ever been in a situation where everything was going fine and in less than a minute, it seems like everything just got shot to hell? You know those situations, where one minute. You and your friend, brother and brother, sister and sister, or husband and wife were all just talking and things fine. Then, all of a sudden you guys are arguing, fighting, cussing each other out, etc.? You know you said one thing and the other person took it the other way or vice versa? All of a sudden things went wrong because of a slight miscommunication or a misunderstanding. All of a sudden things just don't make sense. This is all due to the curious Npu who has the ability to go anywhere. He is the first netchar we all meet. In fact, if you ever go and look at the photos of Tutankhamen's tomb, you'll see standing at the doorway, Npu because he is the guardian of the dead. He is always the first to be honored[22]. He ensures that messages are received on time and that they are interpreted correctly. One of the first stories that illustrate this point is the following Yoruba tale that Papa told me.

Ellegua as the Opener of the Way

One of those stories that explain why he has access to everything is that one day the Divine Creator became ill and he called all of the orishas together to see if they heal him but none could. Then Ellegua (the Yoruba

---

[22] One of Npu's attributes is called Apuat "Opener of the Way," when you read the Story of Osar you find that Oset had problems finding the body of Osar. Her luck changed once Npu began to assist her. Afterwards, she meets some children who point her in the direction the chest of Osar flowed.

142

Npu) appeared and healed the Creator, so to show his gratitude. The Divine Creator told him that he would give him anything he wanted. So, Ellegua said that he wanted to have the freedom to go anywhere he so chooses. The Creator granted Ellegua his wish by giving him a set of keys that could open any door in the universe. From that moment on, the Creator told all of the other orishas that from now on, everyone would have to honor Ellegua before anyone could do anything, because he can open any door (good or bad) and holds in his hands the keys to life and death.

This is the story that helped me to see why Npu was called the Guardian of the Dead. Archeologists will claim that Npu was usurped by Osar only because they don't understand the power of metaphors and don't see that it is our thoughts that determine the type of life we will live. This is the reason why in the *Story of Osar*, Oset could not find Osar's body until Npu came to her side. Soon after she came in contact with some children playing, which are all manifestations of Npu.

Npu is one of the netchar that we all meet regardless if we believe him or not. He makes himself known whenever there is a problem and we learn not do something. This is why I think we all have met him on more than one occasion. I know that I have. Every time I was on the street, on a street corner, he was with me. Every time I had a major decision to make, he was with me. Whenever I grossly err he was right there saying either, "I told you" or "Well, now you know," because he is the messenger of Osar that teaches about life through cunningness. From this perspective, he can be kind and in an instant become cruel and mischievous, which is why Westerners usually mistake him as being the devil. But there is always a lesson to learn behind his feats. Usually, this lesson to be learned is everything is not what it seems, so be careful what you say because there is always another side to the story. The one story that reminds me of this that Papa told me was Ellegua and the Red and Black Hat.

Ellegua and the Red and Black

One of the first stories I heard about Ellegua is that there were two men in a village who were very good friends since childhood. The men were such good friends that each owned a home across from each other, and every morning they would greet each other before working in their fields.

One day Ellegua seeing the great friendship that two men had decided to have some fun with them, so when the two men were outside hoeing and chopping in their fields, he decided to walk down the road between the two wearing his favorite red and white hat, which was red on one side and white on the other. As Ellegua did this he made a loud sound so that to one man it looked like he was wearing a red hat but to the other a black hat (in other versions the hat is red and white).

Later during the day, when the two friends met to eat lunch the two spoke about the mysterious man in the hat, surprisingly the two best of friends began to argue about the color of the hat. The bickering quickly erupted into a fight with the best of friends trading blows. When Ellegua had his laugh, he walked over to the bloodied men who were each demanding to be declared the victor and showed him that his hat was red on one side and white on the other. Shaking his head and chuckling, he walked away amazed that two best friends would be willing to kill each over something so trivial as the color of a hat.

Npu reminds us that life is not just white and black or red but consists of plenty of shades of gray. For this reason, the mischievous spirit's favorite colors are red and black and sometimes red, black and white. In the Afro-Diaspora small images of him are usually kept behind the front door with a toy to keep him entertained and a walking stick, painted white, white and black or red, red, black and white. Everyone has a different view of how this spirits looks. I envision him as a young man with a jackal or dog mask painted in the red, black and white colors. He is fond candy, rum, whiskey, popcorn, fruit, cookies and sweets. In many ways, Santa Claus is an apparition of Npu. His favorite number is 3 and its multiples to 21.

He can be found at every crossroad and at the threshold. He is the personal guardian of everyone, watching us carefully so that he can report what we have done. Although he can be kind and at the same time cruel, he is the spirit that can teach us "tough love" as we move through the stages of life. It is in our moments of uncertainty when we hope that we are making the right decisions in life that he appears. It may all seems like a gamble. If we make the right decision it will lead to us being prosperous, but if it is an unwise decision it may lead to our demise. This is why it is always best to have Npu on your good side, so that we are led in the right direction and if we happen to go down the wrong path. We hope that our lesson learned is not too harsh, but quick.

Another story, which Papa relayed to me, was how this busybody spirit has a tendency of causing trouble at bars and nightclubs. Was that usually the only one up in the middle of the night is Ellegua. When Ellegua finds that someone is up at the bar he goes in and causes trouble between Chango and Ogun. Usually the scuffle between these two hot and masculine orishas begins because Oshun is usually with the harsh Ogun, but the orisha of sensuality is in loved with Chango. It won't take long before Chango's passionate glance meets with Oshun's and the two end up interlocking in some form of embrace. Naturally this angers Ogun who confronts Chango and the two ends up fighting. Next thing you know, Ochossi comes in and carts everyone to jail, while Npu who escapes unscathed sits in the corner laughing at the trouble he caused.

Usually the first thing that a Western trained mind wants to understand is why would Npu do this? Why would he want to create mischief just for his enjoyment? And, this is how we lose sight of him and he falls back into the backdrop laughing. The point of the above stories is not to explain how and why Npu exist, but to accept that he does and failure to recognize him is how mischief is created. If it helps, you may want to think of his as being like child that is always getting into trouble if not entertained. To me Npu reminds me of what the old people use to say, "That an idle mind is the devil's workshop" and in regards to Npu. If he is not given a task he can easily wonder off and you will find him playing in TASETT. This seems to happen to me from my personal experience. I know especially when he is not honored that's when it seems like things seem to always come up missing.

Honoring Npu

To keep Npu entertained and prevent him from wandering off and causing mischief, it is customary in many Afro – Diaspora traditions to honor this Mercurial entity on a weekly or monthly basis to ensure that he keeps the roads open for you, and closes the door to those who would do you and your loved ones harm. When the way is open miscommunication, misunderstandings, etc. are less likely to happen. He simply guides you to your destination safely and you can return safely. When you have a connection with Npu, he will make his presence known to you in a very direct way. For instance, one of the toys that I have for my Npu I found outside in front of my house. It was a red and black Hummer with chrome wheels. I remember saying to myself that my Npu likes to travel in style. I picked the toy up, blessed it and placed it on his het. This is how I know that Npu if he is not entertained he will wander off and you will find yourself going down the wrong path.

Working with Npu

Although Npu is very mischievous his whole purpose in a roundabout way is to help us to see that anything is possible when we put our mind to it. Usually when the way is closed meaning nothing seems to work the way we want it to, it is because we are only seeing one side of the picture. To open the way you need to write out what it is that you really want. If for instance, you want a job but the reason you want a job is so that you can get some money to put food on the table. Then what you really want is not a job or money but food on your table. This is what you need to write down. Once you have this written down, light a candle and ask Npu to help you to get what you want. While the candle is burning daydream and contemplate on what you want coming to fruition. Don't worry about how it will happen, just be thankful and expect that it will. When you have thoughts of doubt that enter into your awareness regarding your goal, you must ignore them and imagine being happy and enjoying your goal. When Npu assists you in your objective make sure that you pay him his just due.

Hruaakhuti, Guardian of Iron

Hruaakhuti is the guardian of iron and the warrior against evil. I have heard some say that Hruaakhuti is the netchar of war, but since war brings calamity, chaos and destruction I disagree and see Set as the spirit of war. Hruaakhuti is the one that challenges Set and fights to bring it to an end. In this sense, Hruaakhuti is the one that triumphs over adversity. Although most martial archetypes tend to have mood swings from a calm disposition to a violent outburst. The Kamitic Hruaakhuti is typically a, no nonsense, cold-blooded warrior for justice incapable of forgiving offences. Think of a perfect samurai with excellent discipline and you would have Hruaakhuti, which is a force that knows exactly what and where to wield his blades.

Usually a lot of people try to stay away from Hruaakhuti because of his absolute honesty, which makes him appear to brutish. With most people when it comes to Hruaakhuti, they either like him or they don't.

146

For instance, while you may cry on Oset's or Nebhet's shoulder when things aren't going well, this is not the case with Hruaakhuti. He will tell you what it is that you need to know rather you like it or not, in the most shocking way possible. If you want to see Hruaakhuti in action, watch a video recording of Malcolm X when he began to make a public appearance on television. When it comes to Hruaakhuti it is black and white, no gray areas in between. You are either right or wrong and if you are wrong watch out you are about to get hit.

Hruaakhuti and Exercise

I remember the first time I met Hruaakhuti and recognized that it was him, which has influenced the way I live today. I was called to jury duty, which should have been my first sign since Hruaakhuti stands with Maat. I was young. I had read and studied just about everything I could get my hands on, so I was feeling pretty good about myself. Ok, I really had a big head and felt like no one could tell me anything because I was a spiritual intellectual.

Anyway, I was called to jury and like most people I tried to get out of it for one because my car was broke and I didn't want to have to catch the bus to go downtown, but I couldn't get out. So I report in and when I get there. There was a room full of people waiting to be selected, so I go and sit down and began reading a book I had, which was on metaphysics. Because the waiting room I was in was a little noisy I went to a nearby room and there was this other guy who looked about thirsty that followed after me with a book in his hand as well. So, there are a few of us in this room then out of nowhere, this guy looked at the book I was reading and commented on it. He then showed me the cover of his book, which was about the kabbalah and from there we began talking. We talked for the entire morning about everything from metaphysics, history, religion, spirituality, etc. Then, he invited me to eat with him in the cafeteria and offered to pay for my lunch. As we continued to talk about everything under the sun it seems, out of nowhere he tells me that I have a good head on my shoulder. That I have the science and spiritual aspect down and that I am going in the right direction.

Then he looked me straight in the face and told me that physically I was not doing well. He told me that I was not exercising nor was I taking care of the physical like the Kamitic people had done. He then told

147

me, that if I looked at any of the Kamitic statues and wall carvings that there were no overweight people. Also, told me that Kamit was not an impoverished country, but the way I was living does not coincide with what they believed. He then proceeded to tell me that he was actually in his 40s and how he runs sprints, which today is considered a vital element of high intensity training. So, he ended with I need to do better in dealing with the physical

What was interesting about this was that I didn't know this man but somehow he knew that I was not exercising like I should have been, and that my funds weren't like they were supposed to be, because I was wasting money. He basically busted my ego. After we had finished lunch, the bailiff came in and told us that the case was dismissed and that we were free to go, which meant I was supposed to meet this man and hear this message. Here this total stranger dropped me back off at my house and we exchanged numbers. A week later when I called him, he didn't know who I was and didn't even remember meeting with me, so I knew this is how I know today that the netcharu work through strangers and that it was Hruaakhuti who had visited with me.

The point of the story is that Hruaakhuti is a warrior when it comes to working with him. It is hard to be a warrior if you aren't prepared to do so physically.

Conspiracy Theory and Hruaakhuti

There aren't many stories that Papa told me about Ogun, whom he called Sarabanda at time, except for the fact that sometimes he doesn't get along with Chango, but then when he does they are awesome fighters that work together to defeat the devil during a thunderstorm (Set). Other than that, I basically learned that Ogun is the energy of hard work and the patron of construction workers, soldiers, surgeons and the master of technology which he uses to improve all aspects of life. As the guardian of iron, he should stand next to front door. At the time, I remembered I could never figure out why Papa kept this big iron pot behind his front door and how was it going to protect his house (yeah, typical Western thinking). I later learned that it attracts warrior spirits. When I asked why someone needs warrior spirits he told me that regardless of what "spiritual people" may claim. There are people in the world that are meant to do you harm. You can be as nice as you want to them. You can help them out in times of

148

need and doing everything that a righteous individual should do and if these people get a chance. They will try their best to harm you and your loved ones. The fact is that there are people like this and fortunately Ogun exist to subdue our enemies, but this does not mean you are supposed to worry about it.

I mentioned before that when I was younger I use to be real big into conspiracy theories. I am not sure how I got into them. All I know is that one day I was a pretty free going individual and the next thing I know I didn't trust anyone, especially not the government. Then one my father told me to go to our neighbor's house to see if we could borrow some of his tools.

Now our neighbor whom I will call Mr. J was a pretty decent guy. He lived alone and worked as a boiler operator at one of the auto plants in Detroit. He had a good job and apparently enough money to have a car and a motorcycle, but he was always alone. We always wondered why he was alone but no one never really inquired about it. Then, on this particular day that I went over to his house to borrow some tools I learned why.

When I went into his house, it was very clean. He had just finished cooking, so his house was full of a heavy aroma of garlic, onions and bell peppers. Anyway, as we went down the stairs to get the tools we needed, he took me into his den, which had the best entertainment system I had ever seen during that time. Alongside the wall were neatly stacked videotapes of various conspiracy plots. He was watching one of the tapes, which I found to be very interesting. When he saw that the program on the television peak my interests. Mr. J. began telling me how the government was doing this, that and the other. All of it was very interesting, but one theory seemed to wrap around another and then another and another and so on. When I looked around, I saw he had a pretty large library of videotapes on the subjects and a number of books. When I finally saw my chance, I told him that I had to get these tools to my father and I politely excused myself.

I never went back over to Mr. J's house anymore. Although what he was talking about was very interesting I just couldn't bring myself to do it anymore, and it wasn't because what he was talking about didn't make sense. Some of it but some of what he said just didn't compute. A year or so later, he had married his high school sweetheart who had a couple of boys. About a year or later, they were divorced. When he had talked to my father I overheard him telling my father that it just didn't work out. One of the things that didn't work out was that she was a church going lady and he believed that religion was used to suppress the masses.

About the same time, that's when I was getting into conspiracy theories I happened to catch myself when I realized that I was becoming like Mr. J. I had noticed that after reading so many books that religion was used to control the masses, but a part of me still believed in God. A part of me read about how smallpox blankets were given to the Native Americans; how 600 impoverished African American with syphilis (around 200 of them did not have the disease prior to the experiment) were not treated for the disease for the sake of science in the Tuskegee Experiment. I read about the sterilization of Puerto Rican women during the 1930s and 1970s. I read about the total destruction of cities like Rosewood and heard from eye witnesses about how they heard the bombs destroy Black Wall Street in Tulsa, Oklahoma, and little to no justice was served, and it all made me angry as hell. But, it made me also realize that if I followed down this path I would be like Mr. J. lonely and fighting alone. I remember this troubled me because it made me wonder how in the world you could survive where the enemy is far stronger and has more resources than you. It wasn't too long afterwards I came across Jacob H. Carruther's classic *The Irritated Genie* and learned about the Haitian priest Boukman Dutty who presided over the ritual made a blood oath to Ogu (the Vodun Hruaakhuti), which many slaves, ex-slaves and *free gens de couleur* (free men of color) participated in, that led to the Haitian Revolution.

In 1804 inspired by the French Revolution Haiti became the second nation in the Western hemisphere to declare its independence following the United States. It was the first black republic and the first nation to declare its independence in the Caribbean and Latin America. Since that time due to unfair racial policies imposed on it by its last occupiers the United States, which crippled Haiti's economy. Combined with the three day genocidal spree by Dominican Republic Rafael Trujillo, the cruel dictatorship of the Duvaliers, followed by various other calamities, Haiti the inspiration to many has become the poorest nation in the Western hemisphere. While everyone has his or her beliefs as to why Haiti fell and is still trying to stand, my take on the subject is that if the legend is true and everyone on the hot night in August took a blood oath

150

to Ogu for freedom. It is the leaders of Haiti that apparently broke this oath to Ogu and, they are the ones responsible for Haiti's downfall.

You see, Hruaakhuti is about doing what is right even when no one is around. He is the one that fights for us when our enemies out number us 10 to 1. Although, I didn't go into detail, when the Haitians declared their independence and fought for their freedom. They didn't just beat Napoleon's military once but a couple of times, which led to the Louisiana Purchase. The leaders of Haiti didn't honor their oath, so Set consumed them. When they should have been doing what is right, they took the easy road and made a deal with Set.

You see, what I got from the history of Haiti is that Hruaakhuti fights for the just, but when you begin committing offenses you have just put yourself in the unjust category. It is a common habit we are all guilty of doing every now and then. For instance, just because no one is looking do you steal paper from your job or run copies off without permission? Do you run the traffic light or stop sign because there are no police around? Do you steal money out of the cash register when no one is looking? If you are guilty of doing any of this you are committing an offense against Hruaakhuti and no amount of rationalizing is going to make it any better. If you are stealing to get back at someone for doing you wrong you have just taken justice in your hands. You are saying that you know how to serve justice better than Hruaakhuti. Think about that? That means someone does you wrong on the job and Hruaakhuti may have set it up so that you got a promotion and was that individual's boss, but you let Set tell you to get them back by stooping to their level.

In this "Get Yours" thinking society we live in now, it is all about getting what you want but by taking advantage of others. This only encourages Set to fully take control, because if it is desperate means that leads you to commit one crime. What happens when the situation becomes even direr? Answer, you commit even more heinous acts. It is like telling a lie. Once you tell one you have to tell another and another to cover up for the previous ones. This is why Hruaakhuti is a warrior and comes in and ends it all. If you are going to do right, you do right period. You suck it up, bite down and do what is right.

But most people want to do what is right. The thing is that they are like Mr. J. afraid that someone is going to abuse, misuse or take advantage of them. This is what most people are trying to avoid, because no one likes being had, but the truth is. The basis of this behavior is fear and if you live in fear you have already been taken advantage of. This is why most of the revolutions that were loss were due to some traitor. The traitor didn't betray his or her comrades because they thought they were going to be successful. They did it out of fear. If Boukman Dutty would have only told the people about the *Story of Osar*, it could have been foretold that the corruption in the government most likely was going to be an inside job. Isn't this how Set killed Osar, it was an inside job? Hopefully, Haiti would have learned its lesson and finally will rise up as the jewel it was meant to be in the Caribbean.

So how do you keep from being taken advantage of? The only way that I know of is to trust your *ba* and do what is right even when no one is around. When you have committed a wrong you need to cease from engaging in the act or behavior and make amends because Hruaakhuti is all about "True Justice" or that real karma. You know like the stockbroker that embezzles everyone's money and seems to go away unscathed, because they have a good lawyer on their side. They can break manmade laws but they can't break Maa and the punishment is on its way due to their conscience.

Working with Hruaakhuti

Hruaakhuti does not start chaos, confusion or war, Set does. Hruaakhuti on the other hand fights to bring it to an end. When Hruaakhuti enters the space it is all about what is right and what is wrong. He comes to even the playing field and make life fair. There's a bit of immediate karma that comes to play when working with Hruaakhuti. He will assist anyone in any of the endeavors that he governs, but he favors the individual that works the hardest for what they want. To work with Hruaakhuti requires that you get up and move! You need to write down what you want! Imagine having it right now!

Now focus on what you have to do to keep it! For instance, if you are a student trying to get A's in your class, change your perspective and imagine already having an A's, now think what you have to do to keep that letter grade. If you want to lose weight, imagine the ideal weight you want to be and live your life as if you are already in shape. Write down all of the things you would do if your goal was already achieved and you were

152

trying to maintain it. Next, make a commitment that you will not cease until you have achieved your objective.

After you have made your commitment, light a white candle to Hruaakhuti and ask for his assistance in the matter. This shift in perspective should cause you to abandon old habits and patterns that deter you from your goal. Continue to do the above steps until the desired results have been obtained. When you see signs that your situation is improving make an offering of his special foods.

Often times when people work with this energy they believe that it means that you are supposed to be overly abusive, aggressive and mean to others in order to get ahead, but this is not Hruaakhuti, that's Set. Hruaakhuti is about doing what is right and what is just. If you steal from someone, someone is bound to steal from you. If you cheat, you will be cheated when you least expect it because this is the Maa. Hruaakhuti comes to teach you that on the flipside if you work hard, do right by others, do what is right even when no one is looking, you will receive your just reward. When it comes to working with Hruaakhuti you must resist the urge to follow your *sahu* impulses because this will lead to Set. This is the purpose behind making a commitment to Hruaakhuti. To gain his assistance in overthrowing the influences of Set and the aapepu, write down on a white sheet of paper all of the ideas and thoughts that come to mind trying to sway you to follow the wrong path. Light a red candle and take the paper and stick it to a dagger, knife or machete. Next ask Hruaakhuti to assist you, and then safely burn the paper in front of his image. Imagine as the paper burn doing what is right and just even in the face of opposition. Repeat this ritual until you see the desired results.

Maat, Guardian of the Maa

Maat governs the weighing of the heart proceedings. She helps us to keep our *ab* guilt free. Maat is the personification of the Maa. In this regard she is the interpreter of the Maa and the patron of the police. Some people may disagree with this manifestation but if you have ever been pulled over by the police. It is basically their interpretation of the law that will determine if you get a ticket or worse. In fact, years ago this is what people use to call the police, "The Law." It is this understanding that led me to identify Maat with the Christian martyr John the Baptist.

153

According to the Gospel of Luke, John was the son of Zechariah a Jewish priest and his barren wife Elizabeth, whose birth was foretold to his father by the angel Gabriel. There's not much mentioned about John except that he was the cousin of Jesus that preached and baptized individuals. According to some scholars they believe that John was an ascetic most likely influenced by the Essenes who preached an apocalyptic message at the River Jordan. Whatever the case, John is remembered for first baptizing Jesus and second for his memorable death. In Mark 6.14, Herod imprisons John for denouncing the king's incestuous marriage to his brother's former wife and niece, Herodias according to the Old Testament Law. When Herodias's daughter Salome danced before her stepfather and great-uncle, she offered him a favor and in return asked that John the Baptist be beheaded.

Maat does what is right and just regardless of the consequences. She does what needs to be done to restore balance to the equation. Maat is a very merciful netchar whose protecting hands can keep anyone safe from harm even in the midst of a storm, because Maat is about strengthening our faith in our own divinity. She is the one that guides us through the storm when we can't see what lies ahead. She is the original Lady Luck who governs the celestial body Jupiter. It was Maat's faith and mercy that led me to identify her with Saint Sebastian.

The Legend of St. Sebastian

Legend has it that Sebastian had everything going for him. He was the son of a wealthy family. He was educated, privileged and a number of opportunities. When he grew up, he a captain in the Imperial Roman army and had befriended the Emperor Diocletian. At the time the emperor despised Christians and he began vicious campaign to persecute and execute all who rejected God. Although no one knows when Sebastian converted to Christianity or if he converted to the new faith at all, legend has it that he secretly would take supplies to comfort those who had been victimized. Sebastian's bravery is said to have converted other soldiers to the new religion who saw that his faith was more important than his life. When he was discovered, Emperor Diocletian asked him to deny his faith, which Sebastian refused to do. So, the emperor had him taken outside, tied to a tree, shot with arrows and left for dead. To the emperor's surprise, Sebastian did not die. When he recovered from his wounds, he returned to the emperor's presence and began to preach to him, but the angry emperor had Sebastian clubbed to death.

154

Sebastian's legend grew during the 14th century Great Plague that devastated Europe. Because of the unpredictable nature of the plague people compared it to being shot by an archer's arrows, so in desperation. People prayed to Sebastian to intercede on their behalf.

It is Maat that allows people from all walks of life to succeed in life even in the gloomiest situations. She works with Npu to give us an out when there is none available. When an opportunity appears out of nowhere this is Maat's doing, but don't mistake her kindness for blindness. When she presents an opportunity you need to take advantage as soon as possible before Set closes the way with his doubt.

Working with Maat

Maat is the netchar that gives us a change of heart. She sympathizes with us and gives us a break, but she is not a push over. You can't just bat your eyes and expect her heart to soften. Her compassion is not like Oset and Nebhet. No, you have to convince her that you are at least trying before she will assist you. You have to be going the right way before she can give you a chance. To work with Maat requires a real extension of faith and a bit of optimism. First, you will need to write down what you want Maat to assist you with. Fold it up and give it to her. Next light a white candle and live as if it has already been achieved by giving thanks for what you already have and what to come. Make a commitment to maintain an optimist attitude be expressing your gratitude for all of the good things that you have (not what you want[23]) in life. Continue to do the above steps until the desired results have been obtained. When you see signs that your situation is improving make an offering of his special foods. Once your objective has been obtained be sure to give her a special offering.

Like Hruaakhuti, Maat requires that you do what you know is right. She is very ethical and understands that occasionally we all bend the law, but if this is done constantly you are breaking the law. If you know something to be right it doesn't take someone passing a written law for you to obey it. Live righteously. The same goes for following your maa. If something doesn't work for you, stop forcing it. Accept that it doesn't

---

[23] Remember the *sahu* is very logical and honest. It knows when it is being lied to, so to say that you are grateful for something you don't have will cause it to become suspicious.

work for you and follow your maa, which should not bring or cause any harm to you or anyone. If you need assistance finding your maa refer back to the Seven Codes of Maa, follow your *ba* and refer to the maa aankh.

Sokar, Guardian of Illnesses and Infirmities

Sokar is the netchar that gives us the will to survive. He is teaches us how to cope with our misfortunes, shortcomings and suffering especially illnesses and diseases. He tempers our will and makes it strong like steel, so that only the mature and strong survive, and witness the awesome power of the Divine.

I learned about Sokar through a variety of sources. I remember when I first met Sokar. It was through his identification of him as the Santeria orisha Babaluaiye in his Catholic guise as the statue of St. Lazarus saintly dressed in purple regalia. I remember hearing Desi Arnaz sing about the orisha of illness and pestilence but I hadn't made a connection with him yet. Then, I remembered hearing Elvis Crespo's pay homage to this orisha in his Luna Llena (Full Moon) and remembered thinking of Papa's St. Lazarus statue and wondering, "Why would anyone want to pay homage to a frail, sickly man?" Then the answer came to me in very strange way. One day while watching television they showed on the WorldLinkTV station the Buena Vista Social Club, featuring one of my favorite Cuban singers Ibrahim Ferrer. As crew documented the singers and the numerous obstacles they had to overcome to make this project a success. They interviewed Ferrer who had a shrine dedicated to guess who. That's right Babaluaiye, whom he referred to as his Lazaro (Lazarus). The sacred space was very rustic but very majestic, then Ferrer when talking about Lazaro said and I am paraphrasing, "Lazaro opens the way for when there are difficulties ahead." In other words, he helps people to succeed when they have to struggle.

When I became ill, I erected a little space for him but the netchar still had not made his presence known to me. I still didn't have a lot of knowledge on who he was and how to obtain his assistance. I looked for his Kamitic imagery but it was archaic and depicted him as being over death. I wasn't trying to die. I needed something to help me to survive, so I purchased a small St. Lazarus statue, but I wasn't sure which Lazarus I had. Was this the Lazarus from the parable Jesus spoke of or the Lazarus that was made whole again after being ill? I wasn't sure and it was, but it was very important that we had the right one because they are worked differently. Then, having problems walking up and down the stairs, I decided to try something, so I removed my Lazarus' crutches. Shortly after, I was able to walk and through practice I began walking up and down the stairs but something was still missing. Then, that's when Sokar made himself known to me. All of a sudden, out of the blue it just came to me. "Sokar is Job." When I realized that Sokar is Job it all made sense. I now had a role model to help me to overcome the illness.

The Story of Job

In the book of Job, there lived an extremely righteous man named Job, who was a very prosperous and wealthy man that owned 7000 heads of sheep, 3000 camels and 500 donkey and oxen. Job with his loving wife had seven strong sons and three beautiful girls, whom he was unhappy with because they did not believe as Job believed, but he loved them just the same. It was apparent that Job was truly blessed, he prayed for his family and he thanked God every day for his blessing. Constantly fearing that the transgressions of his children would anger God, he routinely makes burnt offerings according to Old Law to appease God. Then one day Satan came to God and told him that the only reason Job was so appreciative of God was because God favored him. The deceiver claimed that if God were to relieve Job of his blessing, Job would surely curse God. God assured the devil that Job being a faithful servant would not curse him but the devil persisted. So to prove to the devil that God was right, God gave Satan permission to test Job's righteousness.

All of sudden, all of Job's possessions were destroyed. The Sabeans stole all of his donkeys and oxen, and most of his servants were killed. The Chaldeans stole his 3000 camels. Then a great fire fell from the sky and killed off all of his sheep. Next a mighty wind, the house where all of Job's children was in collapsed and killed all of his offspring. Job looking at all of the calamity occurring around him, refused to curse God but instead shaved his head, tore his clothes and say, "Naked I came out of my mother's womb. Naked I return. The Lord gives and the Lord takes away. Blessed be the name of the Lord."

Then Satan realizing that Job is indeed very righteous asks permission to inflict Job's body. God grants Satan permission but tells him not to take his life. So, Satan smites Job with boils that were so dreadful that he had to use broken shards of pottery to scratch them. Finally, Job's wife exclaimed to him to just curse God, so that he could die, but Job responds, "You speak as one of the foolish speaks. Moreover, shall we receive good from God and shall not receive evil?" Although, it does not mention it is believed that his wife dies.

Then three friends of Job came to visit and console him. Seeing that their friend was suffering and in pain, for seven days they sat with Job on the ground, without saying anything. Finally, since all of the calamities began on the day of his eldest son's birthday. Seven days later he broke his silence, still refusing not to curse God he instead "curses the day he was born."

God later responds by saying that even though Job does not know these secrets of the universe or how nature was formed, he has demonstrated that he has faith in me (whom he has not physically seen) that I am strong enough to pull in the leviathan with a fishhook. God then restored Job's health and blessed him with a new family. Everything that was taken from Job was doubled.

Working with Sokar

In accordance with Kamitic belief, God is not the bringer of evil, Set is the author of calamity, but we see in this story why God allows Set to exist? Why? It is simple, without adversity and obstruction we would be weak. Set is our test and TASETT are the proving grounds, but Sokar is the one to shows us how to Ace the test the Set throws in our ways. It requires of course, that you have a strong faith and a strong will. When we're inflicted with an affliction or some other calamity, sometimes it is best to not even ask "Why it happened?" or "Why me?" This only causes us to naturally focus more on the problem instead of the solution. Once you start focusing on the problem, you become overwhelmed and begin to think about what you can and cannot do. This is when Set wins. You have to focus on the solution, have faith and a strong will that you can burrow through any mountain.

To work with Sokar you need to write down everything you believe you can't do in regards to your objective as it pertain to Sokar. For instance, if you feel that you will not be able to walk because the doctors and other specialists said that you couldn't base upon their findings. Then you need to write this down. Write everything that you believe you can't do related to your objective.

Now, make a commitment that you will not say you can't, but instead will believe that you can achieve your goal. In fact, I have found it best to erase this concept from your mind totally based upon the Codes of Maa and change the perspectives totally. For instead of trying to recover from an illness, switch the situation around and look at it as what you would do to stay healthy. I remember the first time I came across this little technique, it felt like when I said affirmations to better my health. My *sahu* was like, "Well, apparently you wouldn't be saying 'I am healthy,' if you were healthy already." I couldn't argue with my *sahu's* reasoning. Healthy people don't say affirmations or pray for healing, only people that have ill-ness. It is the same for people who want to get in shape through diet and exercising. I have never heard of people who were in shape say an affirmation that they want to be in shape. They simply believe they are and workout to maintain their physique. The same attitude has to be taken in regards to everything else and Sokar is the one helped me to realize it. As I mentioned in earlier and in the *MAA AANKH*, when you focus on doing something to prevent something like losing your money, getting sick, etc. you are putting energy into something your fears. Understand, I am not saying that affirmations don't work. If they worked for you great, I am just offering a different perspective on a common problem based upon my experience.

After you have made your commitment, light a white candle to Sokar and ask for his assistance in the matter. Continue to do the above steps until you see a change. When you see signs that your situation is improving make an offering of his special foods.

When working Sokar, you might get the idea to stop associating with certain people, to turn off the television or abstain from a particular action, beverage or food. This is because Sokar is very austere and wants you to take the issue serious. If you do a ritual to him he wants you to work unceasingly (pray without fail) and spend every moment you can spare working with him, even your leisure time, because he can become a bit jealous. Working with him is sort of like learning how to ride a bike. You keep trying and trying and trying until you can ride the bike yourself without any training wheels. Once you get it, you can never ride a bike in 15 years but, if you pick it up you will know how to do it. In many ways Sokar is associated with our long term memory.

I must state this for the record so that we are clear. The information contained in this book is intended to be educational and not for diagnosis, prescription, or treatment of any health disorder whatsoever. This information should not replace consultation with a competent healthcare professional. The content of the book is intended to be used as an adjunct to a rational and responsible healthcare program prescribed by a licensed healthcare practitioner. This is all about faith, which as I stated before is not based upon what you believe but what you know. All illnesses are due to stress and it is stress that causes imbalance. You cannot totally get rid of stress because you need it in order to live, but you can learn how to manage and minimize it. The easiest way to do this is first, by trying to get at least seven to eight hours of sleep. Second, try to eat a wholesome, nutritious and stress free diet, meaning your food is supposed to provide you with fuel and nourishment first and lastly delight your palette, not the other way around. Third, you need to connect to a state of health by keeping your mind focus only on healing, which means don't read about illness, don't watch television about illness, do not entertain theories about how illnesses occur, do not sympathize with people about their illness, etc. Simply focus on perfect health and when bombarded with people with illness try to if you can lift them up. If you cannot simply excuse yourself because you are not responsible for their healing, they are. You have to do what you need to do in order to improve your wellbeing.

Another thing you must understand is that pain is a part of healing. If you are in pain and you need to take medication to help you to manage by all means do so. However, rests assure that the pain will soon cease because you will be healthy.

Chapter 8:
The Kamitic Tablet Oracle

Knowing that our *ba* will not lead us astray is good news because it means that we can always depend upon it especially in times of need and times of uncertainty. It is what makes divination possible and very valuable asset in our development.

The Purpose of Divination

Have you ever been in a "tough love" situation? Here, you have worked hard to get out of debt, to pay your bills on time. You live on a budget and not beyond your financial means. When you want something you make sacrifices by going without certain luxuries to buy the thing you want. Then, here comes your loved one, your friend or some associate who really needs some money for the third time. They tell you that they are about to have their lights turned off or they don't have any money food or some other excuse. What do you do? Your *sahu* feels sorry for them and wants to help them, but if you help them will they pay you back? Probably not, but what should you do? These are situations that you should take to your *ba*.

First off, while we're on the subject the general rules when it comes to lending money is that you should only lend money that you are not going to miss to people. For instance, if someone asks for $20 and you get paid tomorrow. If they promise to give you the $20 back the next day and they do it. Then no harm done they are good for $20 or more, but if they promise and don't give it back the next day, the following days, weeks, months and years. Well, no harm done either, that individual has just proven that their word was not good for $20 and nothing more. Don't lend money if it is your last $20 to feed your children and you for the month. This is called being selfless and Papa told me that when you are selfless. It is like seeing a boulder chasing a person down a mountain and you decide to get in front of the boulder and have it chase you too. In other words, you take on the burdens of others along with your own.

Now, lending money is a very important in business. Most of the business that exist weren't created through the owner's money or assets alone. They borrowed money from others. If it wasn't from banks, it was from family and friends, but if you can't pay back $20 how is someone supposed to trust you with $5000 or more?

So, when you have to lend money in addition to the above rule there are three guidelines you should follow. When someone asks you for some money the first time, following the above rule lend it to them. If they come back a second time and it is for a similar problem. This individual is not managing their money correctly or doing something wisely. If at all possible you need to tell the individual that they need to do something before the problem gets out of hand, and then lend them the money. If they come back and ask for some money a third time, you need to refuse to give them any money and instead give them a lecture, because clearly they do not have a handle on the situation. This is "tough love" because sometimes we have to fall in order to walk and stand or own. The school of hard knocks is great school that has graduated a number of fine individuals, but if you keep bailing people out they will never learn. Everyone's sun must set at the Ra Atum moment in order for them to rise.

But, returning back to our subject on divination. Let's say this individual has given you a very heartwarming story of how they need your financial help. They have cried and have brought you to tears. Both of you are there with noses running and wads of tissue paper all around you. Your eyes are red and then they ask, well what do you do? This is when you take the situation to your *ba* in divination, which is not moved by emotions. Your *ba* will never lie to you and will tell you straight up because it is looking at the right thing to do, which is its purpose. It will say, "Umm. Sorry to hear that, but No. We can't help you financially."

Divination is not evil or a slight of a hand. It is an actual system used to discover what is unknown. This is why all throughout the ancient world and even the biblical world oracles have been used. Just to cite some examples see:

The problem that most people have with divination stems from the fact that there is a divide that exists between those who understand how divination works and those that don't. Unfortunately, there usually is not enough of the former so all forms of divination are usually seen as fortunetelling device. So, regardless of the question, the one consulting the oracle is looking to predict the future, but when the oracle gives a response that doesn't correspond with reality. They claim that the oracle

162

was inaccurate and fraudulent. Actually it is not that the oracle is fraudulent it is that the oracle is not being used correctly.

I have seen this happen on many occasions and once was a victim of another's abuse of it. I have also seen people try to make predictions on how certain events will occur and fail miserably because of it. Time and time again, people go to the oracle and ask "What should they do?" but God did not give the oracle an *ab*. God gave you an *ab* to decide on what you want to do.

Many people ask questions like the above because they want to avoid problems, which is quite understandable. The issue with this approach is that you can never avoid having problems in your life. There are a lot of people that just want to have a dream and then wake up and go outside and they are rich, but it doesn't work that way. This is why oracles don't work when used this way as well. It is because they are not supposed to predict the future but are supposed to help you to understand the choices that you make and the consequences of your actions. In other words, the oracles give you a picture of how things look if you decide or don't decide to take the present course of action. And, if you look closely you will see it is a dialogue or conversation going on, which is why most oracle readings are vague. They never tell you anything directly, because the conversation is between your *ba*, *sahu* and *ab*.

When you go to the oracle to have a reading what happens is that it is your *ab* that asks the question, your *ba* gives the inspiration and your *sahu* is moved to turn to a specific page (bibliomancy), pull a certain card (cartomancy), or execute a particular throw (sortilege). On a deeper level what happens is that your *ab* (you) state what it is that you want. Your *ba* presents possible solutions to your problems and your *sahu* comments based upon past experiences, which is why there is a certain amount of anxiety and fear usually involved when receiving a reading. The conversation sort goes like this:

> Your *Ab* says, "I want to run for the presidency."
> *Ba* states, "Ok Great. There's a lot of work that has to be done, but it is possible. I'll get on it!"
> *Sahu* states, "Are you crazy? You weren't born with a silver spoon in your mouth. It takes a lot of money. You need connections. You need this and that, "and so on.

163

This is why when you do a reading you have to ask questions that will allow your ba to respond with minimum interference from your *sahu*. For instance, if starting a project you wouldn't ask "Will this project fail?" or "How do I make this project a success," because it gives your *sahu* time to counter with its own limited knowledge. It is best to state, "By taking these necessary steps will this project be successful?" or "Will I be successful if I do complete this step?" By clearing stating what you want to do, the steps you are willing to take and most importantly, phrasing the question in hopes of receiving a positive. You minimize your chances of receiving get ambiguous and rhetorical answers. Possible questions you can ask are:

- Is this the right time to ask for a promotion (pursue this business opportunity, change jobs, get married, etc.)?
- Would it be beneficial for me now to accept this job offer (pursue a relationship with this individual, etc.)?

There are several types of oracles that I am fond of and use because I use whatever is needed to help people find the Maa. I use bibliomancy; the art of randomly opening a book to get an answer to a question, if an individual is comfortable with it. Although most people use this form of divination, by allowing the Spirit or *ba* to guide them to an answer using the bible, it can be employed with any kind of book such as a dictionary or even a magazine. Naturally by using a magazine as a medium would require you to be very acute, while trying to interpret what an advertisement of a bottle of cognac has to do with your question.

I use whatever I feel comfortable with, but if I come across an oracle that I have problems with. I take it as a sign that I am not supposed to use it because it doesn't vibe with my *ba*. It could be that the oracle attracts too many influences or it could be that I am not ready for it and need to receive further training. I don't always know and don't really care, because I know that if my *ba* wants to a message to me it will. So there really is no need to go out looking for an answer to your question, which can also come in the form of a dream – another divination process. All you have to remember is that oracles are just tools. I say this because I have seen some real horrible readings given with some complex and elaborate oracles. I have also seen some real good readings with just flipping a couple of coins. I could have easily walked away saying "Boy those oracles are horrible," but it wasn't the oracle it was the reader. So the effectiveness of all oracles depends upon the user. If the user is using the oracle for negative purpose they will get what they put out. If the user is using the oracle for constructive purposes they will get productive and positive interpretations.

The Kamitic Tablets

One of the simplest oracles, which I introduced in *Kamta: The Practical Kamitic Path for Obtaining Power* was what I called the Fishnet oracle, only because the maa aankh is divided into quadrants similar to that of a net. The Shona divination tablets, and the Kamitic pantheon inspired the following oracle that I have been using lately. It is a basic yes/no oracle but it gives more insight as to how the energy is flowing in the events. Following the *Story of Osar*, since the netcharu are believed to work together as interdependent clans. The heads of the tablets or shells represent the netcharu speaking. It is painted a specific color so that it corresponds to one of the moments of the maa aankh (not the color of the netcharu), while the back or tail of the tablet symbolizes Set and the aapepu's influence. This allows you to get two interpretations at the same time.

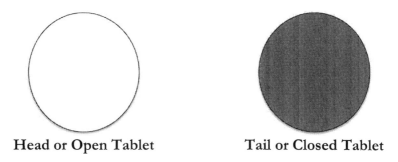

Head or Open Tablet   **Tail or Closed Tablet**

The head or open tablet represents the netcharu (or aakhu) speaking and the tail or closed tablet represents influences from Set.

How to Construct the Tablets

To construct the tablets you need four manageable sized objects of similar shape that can lay down flat on a flat surface. This can be four round coconut discs, four cowrie shells, four flat pieces of wood cut the same length or even four coins. Whatever you use these should small enough for you to put in one hand but large enough to see when it is cast. If using cowrie shells make sure that remove the hump so that the shell lays flat on both sides. Then on the head side of the object you are using, paint one yellow, black, red and white to represent the four moments of the maa aankh. If you cannot paint these sides but prefer to carve them feel free to do so, as long as you can distinguish them from the other.

When your tablets are ready, place the tablets on a white saucer. Then baptize each of them by either:

1. Praying over some water and sprinkle a few drops on each.
2. Praying over some olive oil or some other holy oil and gently dabbing each, or.
3. Spraying them with a mouthful of rum and blowing cigar smoke on them.

Next, light a white candle to your *ba*, netcharu and aakhu and ask that they bless these tablets so that they can communicate to you clearly and offer you no cold readings. Allow the candles to burn out and store your tablets a white cloth. Because you have charged these tablets with your energy, don't let other people use them. These are divining devices and should be stored with other sacred objects.

How to Cast Your Tablets

To cast your tablets, as stated before this is a conversation between your *ba, sahu* and *ab*, so what you are doing is actually creating a way to communicate with your *ba* in a more direct manner. So, the first thing you want is a notebook to keep your readings. To begin, hold your tablets in both hands. Then raise them up towards the sky and then touch the center of your chest to symbolically connect your *ba* and *ab*. Now, say a simple prayer like, "Speak through these tablets *Ba*." While concentrating upon your question, shake the tablets and then cast your tablets. In your notebook, write down the date of the reading, the question and the response.

There are two ways to interpret the tablets. The first is as follows:

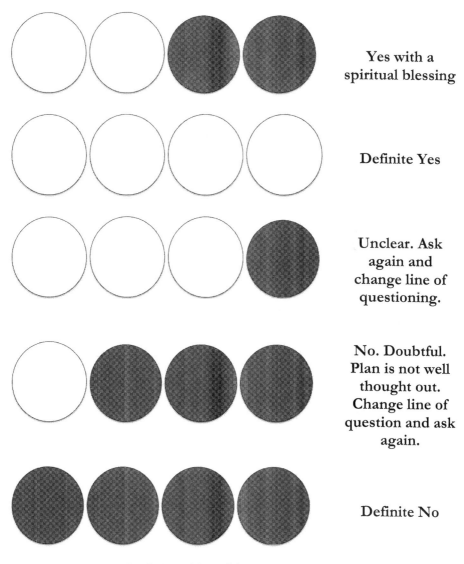

Yes with a spiritual blessing

Definite Yes

Unclear. Ask again and change line of questioning.

No. Doubtful. Plan is not well thought out. Change line of question and ask again.

Definite No

Basic Kamitic Tablet Interpretation

The second interpretation is a commentary to the first response. To understand the second interpretation you have to familiarize yourself with what each of the colored tablets means in regards to the maa aankh.

Amun Ra and the Midnight Moon

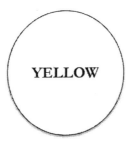

This tablet represents the Midnight Moon and the southern direction on the maa aankh. Since it associated with rebirth, Osar, Sokar and the ancestors speak through it. Consequently, it symbolizes the element of water in all its life giving attributes (rain, snow and semen). In this regard it can bring prosperity and riches into your life in the form of material and spiritual blessings. It is a mature masculine principle, thus symbolizing the man that has seen it all and now lives to tell the story. It is a stern father who displays his power through inner strength and a strong conviction. To get an idea of what this means. Just think of how some animals and people by looking at them. You don't want to try their patience. It is in this sense; Npu speaks through this tablet as the messenger of Osar. This represents the high chief or king, for without him life would not spring forth.

Khepera and Rising Sun

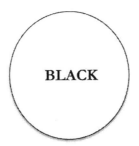

This tablet represents the Rising Sun and the eastern direction on the maa aankh. It is associated with new beginnings and the element of air, hence the color black. Being the symbol of new beginnings it also represents children and the spring season. Since fresh air and is needed for fire to burn. This tablet is associated with the netchar Nebhet and it represents

168

new ideas, artistic talents, luck and innocence, symbolized as Npu. It fans our flames of desire and passion.

Ra and the Midday Sun

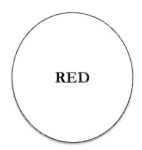

This tablet represents the Midday Sun and the northern direction on the maa aankh, hence the color red. Since this is the most active and hottest time of the day, it is the symbol of health, vigor and one's immune system/defense. It symbolizes the element fire and is associated with Hru and Hruaakhuti. Here the two warriors of fire are working together to defeat Set. They are hot and explosive like flowing lava erupting from the earth or the thunderous lightning shaking the earth, but without any restraints. Just like lava can consume everything in its way and lightning can cause forest fires. So, Maat makes her presence known reminding one the dangers of impetuousness, recklessness and hotheadedness, due to the lack of wise counsel, planning and most importantly balance through self – control. Npu speaks through this sign as a constant reminder to think before you act or speak. Or as my grandfather use to say, "Don't let your mouth get you in something your backside can't get you out of." The modernize version my father use to say is, "Don't let your mouth write a check, your backside can't cash!"

Ra Atum and the Setting Sun

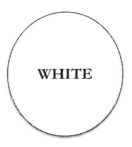

WHITE

This tablet represents the Setting Sun and the western direction on the maa aankh. It is the color white, the color of transformation and change. Metaphorically it symbolizes Oset looking for Osar. Oset is associated with the earth element because she is the one who taught Osar the science of agriculture. She is the one that sown all seeds (physical and spiritual). For this reason, most women in indigenous cultures are the ones that tend to the fields, while men typically tend to the herding of animals. Hidden in this sign is Djahuti offering wisdom on how to achieve one's goal, and also Npu safely guiding Oset in her journey. Since the earth holds life within and only the life giving waters from below can cause it to bring forth life, this is also a symbol of one's home, business and anything that provides the essentials necessary for living. It also represents harvest and therefore, crops and money.

The Combinations Tablets

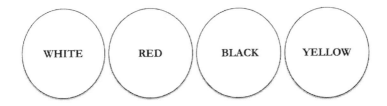

WHITE   RED   BLACK   YELLOW

Midnight Moon, Rising Sun, Midday Sun & Setting Sun – Yes

When all of the tablets are facing heads up. There is perfect harmony, love and knowledge that is present. The two more mature forces are on the outside while the two younger forces are in between. It is the sign of a perfect loving family. All of the forces are working together in support of the objective, but although Set is not seen doesn't mean that he is not present. Remember, Set launched his coup when everything seemed to be perfect. The answer to your question is yes. You have planned correctly, but be on the lookout for surprises. Never get too relax, because this is the time when things can go awry.

The Setting Sun and Midnight Moon – Yes

This is a good combination because here we have Setting Sun and Midnight Moon converging into one. This symbolizes two mature forces – the Father and Mother or Osar and Oset joined as one. Together they bring all of their life experiences and wisdom to address the issue at hand. In order to succeed with your project you will either need to receive good counsel, make a wise decision or will give wise counsel.

The Midnight Moon and Rising Sun – Yes

This combination represents the Midnight Moon and the Rising Sun symbolizing a strong masculine force supporting weak yet creative energy. It is Osar supporting Nebhet, which gives birth to Npu. Something new is on the way. This signs signifies that a new beliefs, new and refresh thinking, new idea, new way of life, new relationship is either required to make your project successful or will be the product result.

The Midnight Moon and Midday Sun – Yes

This combination bridges the present with the past as Hru stands on the other side looking at Osar. This marks the beginning of what could be a very productive relationship, as the two male forces work together for a common goal. Hru with his exceptional leadership skills is able to rally Hruaakhuti and commence to work. Osar because of his knowledge, wisdom and connection with the ancestors, is able to provide the otherwise wayward youth with guidance, so that he does not lose his head. You have to ability to accomplish your desire, but your success depends strongly upon you either developing or combining your leadership, strength and vigor with the guidance so that you do not overdo it.

The Setting Sun and Rising Sun – Yes

In this combination we see Oset and Nebhet working together to recollect the pieces of Osar. This is a quiet combination because the eldest sister is leading the younger. One can imagine as the two (one pregnant or with a baby, the other young and beautiful) travel from place to place, collecting relics and erecting sacred space. They are setting in motion ideas for a revolution. Here the youthful creativity of Nebhet combined with the loving devotion of Oset, combines to create artistic expressions of change. This combination speaks of a new beginning, the promise of a new future. It may express itself in music, dance, poetry or art, whatever the case the child Hru is about to be born. But, the change he will implement will not come quick with this combination. The child still has to grow and until that time comes there will be nothing to energize it. In other words, the seeds of change have not yet been sown, nurtured and given the time to grow. Hru is not of age yet. However, given time the change will occur if you stay the course. Take this time to take it easy, relax and take advantage of the down time. This is not a time for planning but a time for waiting and nourishing.

The Setting Sun and Midday Sun – Yes

Finally, the child Hru is of age and after learning that he can from his mother. He is ready to fight and avenge Osar. In this combination, we see that Oset with her earth attributes has properly fueled Hru's fire. Hru has rallied Hruaakhuti and has begun to challenge Set for the throne. He looks for every opportunity available to better his position. This pattern speaks of advancement in business, career, education and possibly even travel. This combination however also cautions against being overzealous. It was Hru's zeal that led him to cut Oset's diadem, because when fire is not managed correctly. It can get out of hand and instead of fertilizing the ground, it will scorch the earth. Fortunately, Djahuti is present and able to provide wise counsel. Therefore, to succeed with your chosen project, you may need to obtain wise counsel to ensure that your zeal does not overwhelm you and others around you. It is best to get a second opinion just in case you overlooked something.

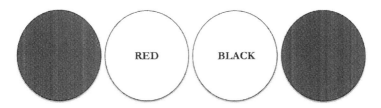

The Rising Sun and Midday Sun – Yes

Here we have the youngest two in the group represented in this pattern. Nebhets creativity and Hru's zeal makes this pattern full of creative energy. Since the air of Nebhet fans the flames of Hru, there is a lot of

173

attraction (fire) in the air. The time and season is right to accomplish nearly any difficulty that stands in your way because the emotions are high. However, with no elder (Osar or Oset) around, youthful and passionate energy without any proper planning can lead to unplanned events. This combination cautions you to think before act.

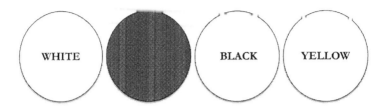

The Midnight Moon, Rising Sun and Setting Sun - Uncertainty

With the two elders Osar and Oset talking and Nebhet standing in between, we see we have a problem. Both Osar and Oset experienced and seasoned but are interrupted by the innocence and naiveté of Nebhet because Set is in front of her. Together a serious imbalance exists, which sets the stage for a storm to ride in on the horizon. Due to Set making his presence known, he causes a disruption in the flow. As a result, Osar's influence is blocked by the more creative and energetic feminine energy being used for destructive purposes. The pattern signifies the possible end of a business, relationship or impending illness, by following the chosen course of action.

The Midnight Moon, Midday Sun and Setting Sun – Uncertainty

Here we have two elders (Osar and Oset) are interrupted by the youthful and zealous Hru standing in between. This time because Set is blocking Osar, thus preventing life giving energy from Osar to getting to Hru. There is nothing to keep the zealous warrior prince from going overboard. Consequently, Hru's fire overwhelms Oset, and scorches the land possibly leading to a flood. Hru is driven to fight but his reasoning in this combination may not be just. Anything could be driving him including fear, false beliefs, or even deception. This combination suggests that at present time your project will fail and someone is going to get hurt (emotionally and possibly even physically). You need to seriously rethink research and get counsel on how to proceed, because you run the serious risk of deluding yourself.

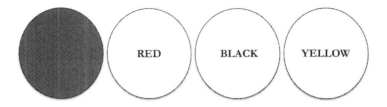

The Midnight Moon, Rising Sun and Midday Sun - Uncertainty

In this combination the inner strength of Osar is present and it supports the creative energy of Nebhet, which fans the zeal of Hru, but he is blocked from advancing by Set. The lack of Oset indicates that there are no resources available. Therefore change cannot occur. In other words, you can't have a revolution without a Mother. The pattern indicates the need for nourishment. At this time you should consider following your *ba* and listening to your aakhu (ancestors). Once this is done, then ask your question again.

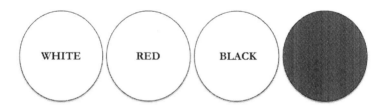

The Rising Sun, Midday Sun and Setting Sun – Uncertainty

In this pattern the creativity of Nebhet is present, the drive of Hru is near and Oset is ready to make change, but the lack of Osar indicates that there is no inner strength and no commitment to change. This is a sign of weakness or one without a backbone. Although there is a lot of potential, the lack of inner strength means there is no ethics, morals, cuff or inner restraint. It has just become a dog war and every man or woman for themselves. This combination paints of picture of lawlessness where deceit, dishonesty and despair run everywhere. Any situation can easily get out of hand due to this sign. If you must proceed do so with extreme caution.

The Midnight Moon – No

In this combination the Midnight Moon tablet is by itself and supported by Set's influence. Here the king is trying to hang on but is easily usurped because he has no assistance. Here we meet a bitter, harsh and oppressive Osar, who although slow has succumb to anger. No one wants to be around him and they definitely don't want to be his subject. Alone this is the symbol of a tyrant who rules with no collaboration or help from others. This is Old Man Winter in physical form, reminding you that no one is island. You have to work with others through the Maa.

The Rising Sun – No

By itself this tablet symbolizes Set's influence, abuse and misuse of Nebhet's ability. It represents naiveté, the misuse of creative power for destructive and negative purposes. Here is where innocence and loss for material gain. It is a reminder to not allow passions to take precedence over our life.

The Midday Sun – No

Basically you are fighting a losing battle alone and in the dark with no guidance, no insight, no committed warriors and no available resources. You have allowed your mouth to get you into a bind and you are stuck on both sides.

The Setting Sun – No

By itself this tablet becomes the barren desert TASETT because of the misuse of earthly resources. When there are no resources death is clearly nearby. At the same time, when there is no love and nurturance in our life, there is no future. Here we meet Oset in the most dangerous and desperate times willing to do anything in order for her child (or family) to survive. She is guided and protected by Npu. Nothing is worse than a mother's fury.

All Blanks Sides Up

A combination means "No!" Whatever you are attempting to do, you need to postpone it because it will not be productive. Set is on a rampage and his agents are on the prowl. Take this time to recuperate, gather your forces and review your plan. If you must proceed, do so with extreme caution.

Additional Subtle Meanings

When throwing the tablets you will notice that the way they fall forms another pattern. Sometimes open tablets will fall on closed ones and vice versa, so the following are subtle answers give additional insight to the readings.

When two open tablets fall together on top of each other and the other two are closed. This could indicate that there is good fortune associated with the question

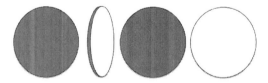

If an open table falls on top of a closed tablet it may indicate that something ominous is coming due to an element associated with the question.

When a closed tablet falls on top of an open tablet it indicates that something blocking the positive forces from coming through. Steps must be taken to remove the closed tablet.

When a tablet lands and it is neither open nor close but rests on its side or edge. It indicates that you need to contemplate on the issue more in depth or see an experienced diviner because you are too emotionally tied to the issue in question.

Chapter 9:
In Its Season the Divine Clock

You know one of the wonderful things about the maa aankh I have learned is that when it is compared to religious texts. It being a cosmogram gives a visual representation of spiritual literature. I remembered as a child that during certain times of the year there were yearly rituals we would do as a family. During the winter months for instance, my mother would give us vitamin C and cod liver oil capsules. In the spring we would sometimes eat dandelion greens and other green vegetables to cleanse our body. My mother wasn't the only one who did these things. Her mother and her friends also followed suit. I thought that one of the interesting things about this was that all of these practices seemed to always coincide with the seasonal changes.

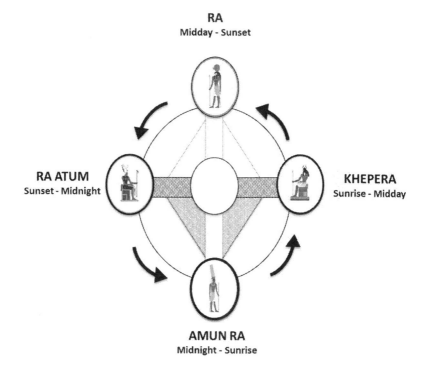

The Maa Aankh Divine Clock

When I got older I learned that some of the elders called these changes that occurred throughout the world God's Clock. God's Clock was different from man's clock because it provided a specific place and time for everything to exist. When one lived in accordance to God's Clock they could minimize the stress in their life. It was for this reason, the elders in my church were fond of paraphrasing was Ecclesiastics 3, "Everything has its season." Listed below are some guidelines based upon the maa aankh to help you in your daily and yearly routines.

Daily Living According to the Maa Aankh

Morning

This is the time of the day when everything is just beginning to heat up. From Sunrise to Noon is overseen by Khepera. Since all of the living things around this time are beginning awake from their sleep. This is also one of the best times of the day to do aerobic exercises or light exercise such as brisk walking on an elliptical machine, treadmill or to work; bicycling, jogging, running in place, running long distance, jumping rope or dancing. Also some sports like soccer, basketball and roller-skating are also good aerobic exercises. Because the body is still waking up it is not the best time to do any anaerobic exercises (like heavy weightlifting, etc.), which is best time around 12 Noon. Besides making most people late for work, when you do heavy lifting in the morning it causes the body to become excessively tired.

You should have a complete breakfast that consists of a complex carbohydrate, protein, calcium and fiber to give you enough energy to make it to lunch. If you are not a vegetarian, allergic to soy products or vegetarian foodstuffs are not easily accessible[24]. You can still have a nutritious breakfast. A typical large breakfast for instance, might consist of one of the following like oatmeal, oat groats, corn meal mush, polenta, corn grits, spinach grits, rice, etc. This could be served with eggs (boiled, poached, scrambled or fried with extra virgin olive oil), poultry (turkey sausage, turkey bacon, turkey chorizo, etc.), seafood (poached fish, grilled shrimp, etc.) or legumes (black beans, pinto beans, garbanzo, etc.), dairy (soy milk, almond milk, ghee, goat cheese, feta, mozzarella, etc. for calcium) and piece of fruit (papaya, bananas, apples, pineapple, etc.).

---

[24] Please note that my intention is to assist you wherever you are in your life and not to sway to follow some particular dogmatic belief. You have to decide what is best for you. If you need assistance please see a licensed dietician or nutritionist.

180

A typical light breakfast can consist of the same items eaten (or grazed) throughout the morning all the way to noon. Coffees, teas and fruit juices are also good to be consumed at this time, but should be drank after consuming a glass of water (preferably lemon water) to help flush your body's systems. Excessive amounts of sugars like donuts, and other sweet pastries should be avoided, since these deserts typically relax us and are opposite of Khepera's energy.

Midday

This is the time of the day when everything is at its highest point of exertion. Ra oversees noon to Sunset, which typically is also the hottest and most energetic time of the day. At this moment everything is in full swing because the energy level is high and at its peak. Ideally this is the best time for eating supper, which should be the largest meal of the day. This for most people is not practical because of our job and busy schedule, which is the reason for having a large breakfast. If you consumed a heavy breakfast you may want to eat a light meal consisting of the same foods. If you consumed a light breakfast you might want to eat a heavy meal. Because most people during this time are on the go, which makes it hard for most to pay attention to what they eat. Convenience and fast foods becomes the most accessible food to eat. Rather than condemn you, I instead would encourage you to make the meal a complete meal. Remember a complete meal should consist of a protein, complex carbohydrate, calcium and fiber. Since most of us when we eat get the protein and complex carb. Try including juice or milk to get your calcium and a nice helping of vegetables and fruit for fiber and nutrients.

This is also the best time of the day to do anaerobic exercises for building strength and endurance. Anaerobic exercises are any exercise that uses resistance to build muscle and power. Anaerobic exercises raise your heart rate on a small scale, accelerates your metabolism, allowing you to burn more calories and 100 % more fat than aerobic exercises, because your body is forced to perform for a short time without oxygen. The most common form of anaerobic exercise is weightlifting (this includes anything with a dumbbell) but, some other simple anaerobic exercises are jumping, pull-ups, push-ups, sprinting short – lasting and high intensity exercises like sprinting, weight lifting or jumping. Some anaerobic exercises, like 50 to 100 rep. no weight squatting, can be done anywhere, because the key is to do one movement as quickly as possible. Be careful that you do not overdo it. You have to rest after doing anaerobic exercises because the body produces lactic acid, which is why the muscles get tired.

Evening

From Sunset to Midnight is governed by Ra Atum. This is the time of the day most people began to relax and unwind. It is also the time of the day that most people eat supper. Ideally the largest meal of the day should be eaten at the Ra moment and before Sunset, but since this is not practical for a lot of people. Try to consume the last meal of the day around Sunset if at all possible, because the energy is waning at this moment. Meals consumed after Sunset on a regular basis are hard for the body to digest leading to upset stomach, indigestion and other digestive related problems along with trouble sleeping. To assist in digestion you might want to consider drinking herbal teas like ginger tea. Light snacks and deserts should only be consumed at this moment of the day and at least three hours before retiring. If you are craving deserts and sweets throughout the day, it may be a sign that your body is not in balance. Your diet may be carbohydrate rich and you are not getting enough protein. As stated before, if you are not able to ascertain the problem see a licensed dietician or nutritionist.

Since the body is trying to relax, this is also the best time to engage in relaxing activities. For the solitary individual yoga and Tai chi might be a practice you want to partake in, but for the rest of us. This is the best time to enjoy family, dance and playing games. That's right turn off the television, relax and play a game with the family. It is also very optimal time for studying, preparing for the next day and retiring to sleep.

When you do retire never go to bed angry or with disturbing thoughts on your mind. Always try to go retire with positive thoughts on your mind. One way to do this is to go to bed while expressing your gratitude for the things you are sincerely grateful for. If you have a job say, "Thank you for my job." Don't say thank you for something you don't like because it sends a message that you want more of the thing that you don't care for.

Midnight

From Midnight to Sunrise is governed by Amun Ra. At this time of the day, most people are sleep. Since Amun Ra governs rebirth, this is the ideal time for doing meditation and spirit work for upcoming events. When one enters into trance during this time they can easily take their trance work into the KAMTA as they fall asleep. This is also the perfect time for husband and wife to have relations, while the home is quiet. It is however, not the best time to be drunk because this is also considering the witching time of the day. All of the spirits (benevolent and malevolent) are believed to roam the earth at this time. The legend that Papa told me relating to Npu being at the bars referred to this time of the day, and it never seems to fail. Most of the situations I have been in where I have seen some type of problem such as two biological sisters fighting each other occurred right around this time.

Celebrating with the Maa Aankh All Year Around

Generally in many climatic areas meteorologist define the four seasons as spring, summer, fall (or autumn) and winter. These four seasons are defined based upon average temperatures that occur on a monthly basis, typically lasting about three months. The coldest months of the year are winter and the warmest months are defined as summer, with the remaining months in between being spring and summer. Since Spring can start on different date, in the northern hemisphere the astronomical spring equinox, the time when the earth tilts on its axis neither toward or away from the sun (around March 20 and 21), is used to mark the first day of Spring, while the autumnal equinox (around September 20 or 21) is used to mark the first day of Fall. For a more up to date listing be sure to check your calendar or Farmer's Almanac.

> Khepera Seasons are spring is March 21 – June 20
> Ra Seasons are summer: June 21 – September 20
> Ra Atum Seasons Autumn: September 22 – December 21
> Amun Ra Seasons are winter: December 21 – March 20
> Note that in tropical areas like Brazil the seasons are reverse[25].

---

[25] Spring: 22nd September - 21st December, Summer: 22nd December - 21st March, Autumn: 22nd March - 21st June and Winter: 22nd June - 21st September

So unlike some Afro – Diaspora practitioners who resent Christianity because of how European powers have used it as a tool of enslavement to promote Eurocentric values, I embrace certain elements of Christianity for several reasons. The first is because as I hope to have shown you, is because the original principles that Jesus taught came from Kamit and second, because. Majority of our ancestors were Christians and are familiar with these principles. As a result, Christianity is nothing more than a medium or language that allows a natural dialog or syncretism to occur. If I were to speak about Hruaakhuti for instance, most people would not know who he is and would not be able to identify with him, unless they were familiar with the Kamitic tradition. If on the other hand, I mentioned the Apostle Peter or Saint George the Dragon Slayer, immediately what comes to mind is the image of a warrior and someone that is about taking care of business.

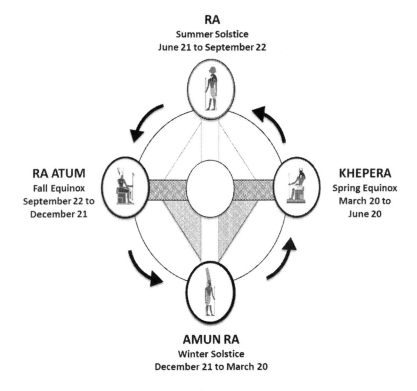

Annual Observation with the Maa Aankh

Simply put syncretism is way a culture survives. So I allow syncretism in my personal practice because I am fond of Afro-Creolized traditions that are practiced in the Caribbean and Latin America. I even acknowledge certain Christian rites. I am not saying that you have to do this, but I do it because it helps me to identify with those who I serve. The astute reader will be able to see why it is easy to draw comparisons between the Kamitic and Christian traditions when using the maa aankh as a guide. For instance, on the 25th of December, I celebrate the birth of Hru, but it is done in a Kamitic way based upon the solstices and equinoxes. The following is a list of annual observances based upon the maa aankh[26].

Khepera Season: Celebrating the Return of Osar
(March 20 – June 20)

At this of the year the planet is beginning to heat up. Everything is starting a new beginning after emerging from the waters of the previous season. Life it seems is starting to return. Trees are beginning to bud, plants are beginning to grow. The days are becoming longer and the nights appear to be shorter. Everything is in a birthing phase, which makes this a great time to do Spring Cleaning for your body and your home. As the days become warmer, pollen is generally high during this time, to avoid allergies and sinus issues. It might be helpful to consume cleansing foods like greens and citrus fruits that help to eliminate toxins and waste from your body.

Around March 20 or 21, marks the spring equinox. Easter is the Christian holiday associated with this event, which is a movable feast, established by the first Council of Nicaea as the first Sunday after the full moon. In Judaism Easter is associated with the Jewish Passover, which according to Jewish "lore" is when the Children of Israel were freed from slavery in Egypt. Now, Papa's syncretism was so unique that he equated Jesus's death and resurrection with Obatala, so on Easter he followed another Creole created tradition, I assume he learned from Cuba. On "Good Friday" (Papa hated the racist undertone in referring to this day as Black Friday), he would place white kerchiefs over his spirits to signify that they were in morning. On Sunday, he would remove these white kerchiefs to signify the resurrection. The fact that this occurred for three

---

[26] Please note this is based upon North American temperate zone.

days was synonymous with his Afro-Cuban beliefs in Ellegua who special number is three.

This is why I am so grateful for this little old man from Cuba coming into my life, because I feel like those who have maintained their traditions throughout the Afro-Diaspora can help those of us who lost a part of our cultural heritage recreate what is sacred to us. I feel that those of us who have lost a lot of our cultural practices in some way feel like we have to have something "authentic" in order to feel good about ourselves. Papa showed me that I didn't. He taught me that so long as I had a firm grasp on the concepts and principles, I don't have to imitate, mimic or steal anyone's rituals or tradition to celebrate who I am. I remember him firmly telling me, (I hope I write this correctly), *"No doy una maldición qué él hace en las otras partes del mundo. Cuido solamente sobre mi manera y qué me conecta con El Hombre arriba.* (I don't give a damn what they do in the other parts of the world. I only care about my way and what connects me to the Man –God upstairs."

You know, we have to celebrate our heritage because it is the only thing that will make us strong and resilient. Of course, before creating any type of new cultural tradition it is always best to consult the oracle to see if your aakhu approve of such a change. Through Papa's inspiration, I follow suit and do the same thing for Osar, which has a strong very significant meaning for me. For me Good Friday signifies the great tribunal between Hru and Set, which was full of doom and gloom due to Set's persuasiveness. It symbolizes the end of Set's tyranny. Easter marks the return of justice, peace, wisdom and the blessings of Osar. This makes it a great time to wear new white clothing.

Ra Season: In Honor of Maat
(June 21 – September 22)

We are entering the hottest times of the year. It is the time when the lack of moisture on the planet and within our body makes us extremely bold, daring and adventurous. Youthful energy at this time of the year is at an all-time high, which means conceptual thinking and commonsense is a mere afterthought. I remember when I use to work for youth programs during the summer, it was considered the worst time of the year because this is when kids got into the most trouble. In fact, during the summer months I remember people use to pray for it to rain because it would force the kids to stay inside and prevent many of them from getting into trouble. I now know thanks to the maa aankh, that this is the time you must always ask what is the right or the Maa thing to do.

This explains the reason why the celebrations that occur around June 21 known in Europe as Midsummer or Midsummer Eve holidays. Typically because those following a lunar calendar began the day at sunset (instead of at sunrise), these pre-Christian holidays and traditions began with the lighting of a bonfire to protect against evil spirits that were believed to roam free after the sun has set in south. Later when Christianity began to settle into these areas, the celebration was associated with the nativity of John the Baptist and idea of being protected from evil spirits was transposed to being purified from sin. As a result, Catholic, Orthodox and some Protestant denominations see June 24 as the official day of celebrating John the Baptist. Historically famous individuals in the Afro – Diaspora like the priestess Marie Laveau, have venerated the date.

When we compare all of this we see that St. John the Baptist corresponds to Maat, which means this time of the year, is about establishing and maintain balance and order. Take a bath asking that Maat bring balance, good luck, order, protection and reveal to us what is not right in our life, so that we are not on the wrong side. If near a beach you may want to dip, into the water twice and leave. If possible you may want to make a two-gallon herbal tea of star anise. When the water has cooled, strain the herbs and pour the cool tea over your head. Afterwards, have a celebration and focus on and what you want to out of life for the next half of the year and give thanks for everything you are grateful for including your health, family, friends, neighbors, community, etc. If you have a party, it should be in Honor of Maat and for a charitable cause. You may be inspired to volunteer your time at your local community center or senior citizen center. Whatever you do, this should be a charitable event, so if money is raised it should be for a good cause. If hosting a party, it should be donations only and the monies given to some charity.

Ra Atum Season: The Great Decline
(September 22 – December 21)

This is the time of the year when the planet is shifting and is beginning to cool. The air is becoming cooler and crisp as autumn sets in. This is the best time to begin storing up on produces by either freezing or canning them for the winter. At this time, it is best to avoid mucous forming foods, which contribute to colds and flu. This is the best time to drink warming drinks like hot, spiced ciders and herbal teas.

Spiritually speaking the autumn equinox is a time of reflection and remembrance. It is a time of listening to your elders, honoring the dead and seeking wise counsel before partaking in future events. The celebrations that occur around this time of the year are usually those honoring the dead. All of the celebrations including All Saints Day, the Day of the Dead, and Halloween (All Hallows' Evening), were all originally created to honor the dead. These holidays came under attack because Protestants rejected the idea of there being a place called purgatory. The other festivals associated with this time are Thanksgiving and the Moon Festival or Mid-Autumn Festival in China and Vietnam.

This is therefore, the best time to honor our aakhu and express our gratitude to them for helping us throughout the year. The best day to do this obviously would be on the 21st of September, the day of the autumn equinox. If this can't be done, then simply pick a day you think is the best day to express your gratitude. Share cultural folktales (not silly ghost stories) with your family and community to teach people not to fear their aakhu and revel in their ancestor's wisdom about life. Consulting your aakhu regarding family issues and the future of the family and be sure to offer them unsalted foods that they enjoyed in life. Remind them that they are missed and that you are still in need of their wisdom. Make this a unique day by wearing special clothes to celebrate your culture such as African attire or ceremonial gowns. The event should celebrate the cultural contributions made to benefit the world and improve the quality of life.

Amun Ra Season: Rise of the King
(December 21 – March 20)

We come what is generally considered the coldest time of the year. In other parts of the world this is the rainiest or a time when you are forced to remain indoors. The nights seem longer at this time of the year and definitely colder. The same dietary advice from the previous season should be followed.

It is the greatest time for contemplation and reflection. This is the time of the year when everything has waned. Historically, this was the most terrifying time of the year because everything seemed to be absent of life, which is why depression, negative thoughts, suicides, etc. are usually high during this time. This particular time of the year is known as the winter solstice is when the sun seems to be standing still; where the sun seems to appear at its lowest altitude above the horizon usually around December 21. Then on the 24th of December, the sun is said to be reborn.

The celebration associated with this event is typically Christmas and immediately following after is Carnival. Typically, I celebrate the birth of Hru by purchasing a nativity scene. The child Hru is also used to represent the return of power and freedom. In this sense, it is associated with the Afro – Diaspora idea of Carnival, the celebration of freedom and abolishing of slavery, as in the case of Dominica, Uruguay, Bahamas and many others.

Conclusion

As usual it was a warm Florida evening but we managed to stay cool as I sat across from Papa and his wife who translated for him, in their little apartment, enjoying the breeze blowing through the windows and open door.

"How do you know if what a person is saying is the truth?" I recalled asking.

"You don't, but you can look at how the individual lives. And, if you what they say is true. Their life will reflect it," Papa answered.

"But, how do you know if what they are telling you will work for you?" I asked.

"You don't. The only way you can tell is by trying out for yourself. If it works then you embrace it as your own. If it doesn't work then there's no loss, you simply move on. So, don't sit up reading a bunch of books and believe everything they say, because most books are just a bunch of theories. If you want to know something you have to try it for yourself and see what works for you. Then that becomes your truth."

I believe that most of the problems that people have could be easily remedied if they made their life revolve around the Almighty. It is because people only see God as existing in a church or temple I believe that causes them not to see God in themselves or in anyone else. Thankfully, it was through this simple wisdom that Papa helped me to see that the purpose of spiritual traditions is to connect you to the Divine.

In our changing world where no one knows what tomorrow will bring, but there is one thing that we do know, and it is that nothing static. Everything is bound to change. Everything is always evolving but concepts and principles will always remain the same. Although you may not know where you will be tomorrow and you may not know what tomorrow will bring. If however, you make cultivating your divinity a way of life, so that you are constantly reminded that you are connected to God. There's nothing you cannot accomplish and nothing you cannot achieve. There will be no need to worry about anything because whatever the future holds you know that you have the ability to accomplish anything.

Selected Bibliography

Ashanti, Kwabena F. *Rootwork and Voodoo: In Mental Health*. Tone Books, 1987

Battle, Michael. *The Black Church in America: African American Christian Spirituality*. Wiley-Blackwell, 2006

Bockie, Simon. *Death and the Invisible Powers: The World of Kongo Belief*. Indiana University Press, 1993

Bolling, John L. "Guinea across the Water: The African-American Approach to Death and Dying." *A Cross-Cultural Look at Death, Dying, and Religion*. Eds. Joan K. Parry and Angela Shen Ryan. Nelson-Hall, 1995. 145-59

Browder, Anthony T. *Nile Valley Contributions to Civilization*. Institute of Karmic Guidance, 1992

Budge, E.A. Wallis. *An Egyptian Hieroglyphic Dictionary Vol. I and II*. New York: Dover Publication, 1978

Budge, E.A. Wallis. *Osiris & The Egyptian Resurrection, vols. 1 & 2*. Dover Publications, 1973

Carruthers, Jacob H. *The Irritated Genie: An Essay on the Haitian Revolution*. Kemetic Institute, 1985

Courlander, Harold. *A Treasury of Afro-American Folklore: The Oral Literature, Traditions, Recollections, Legends, Tales, Songs, Religious Beliefs, Customs, Sayings and Humor of Peoples of African Descent in the Americas*. New York: Marlove and Company, 1976

Diop, Cheikh Anta. *The African Origin of Civilization: Myth or Reality*. Lawrence Hill Books, 1989

Doumbia, Adama and Naomi Doumbia. *The Way of the Elders: West African Spirituality & Tradition*. Llewellyn Publications, 2004

Dossey M.D., Larry. *Recovering the Soul: A Scientific and Spiritual Approach*. Bantam, 1st ed. 1989

Dundes, Alan. *Interpreting Folklore*. Indiana University Press, 1980

Fatunmbi, Falokun. *Iwa-Pele: Ifa Quest the Search for the Source of Santeria and Lucumi*. Original Publications, 1991

Fu-Kiau, K. Kia Bunseki, *African Cosmology of the Bantu-Kongo: Principles of Life & Living*. Athelia Henrietta Press, 2001

Gadalla, Moustafa. *Egyptian Cosmology: The Animated Universe*. Tehuti Research Foundation; 2nd. ed. 2001

Gomez, Michael. A: *Exchanging Our Country Marks: The Transformation of African Identities in the Colonial and Antebellum South*. The University of North Carolina Press, 1998

Hall, James. *Sangoma: My Odyssey Into the Spirit World of Africa*. Jeremy P. Tarcher, 1994

Hollenweger, W. J. *The Pentecostals: The Charismatic Movement in the Churches*. Augsburg Publishing House, 1972

Hurston, Zora Neale. *Moses: Man of the Mountain*. University of Illinois Press, 1984

Ions, Veronica. *Egyptian Mythology: Library of the World's Myths and Legends*. Peter Bedrick Books; Rev Sub ed., 1983

Jacobs, Claude F. and Andrew J. Kaslow. *The Spiritual Churches of New Orleans: Origins, Beliefs and Rituals of an African-American Religion*. The University of Tennessee Press, 1991

Kardec, Allan. *The Spirits' Book*; Kessinger Publishing, LLC, 2003

MacGaffey, Wyatt. *Custom and Government in the Lower Congo*. University of California Press, 1970

MacGaffey, Wyatt. *Religion and Society in Central Africa: The BaKongo of Lower Zaire*. The University of Chicago Press, 1986

Mbiti, John S. *Introduction to African Religion*. Heinemann, 1991

192

Mbiti, John S. *African Religions & Philosophy*. Heinemann, 1992

Paris, Peter J. *The Spirituality of African Peoples*. Augsburg Fortress Publishers, 1994

Puckett, Newbill Niles, *Magic & Folk Beliefs of the Southern Negro*. Dover Publication, 1969

Raboteau, Albert J. *Slave Religion: The "Invisible Institution" in the Antebellum South*. Oxford University Press, 1978

Shafton, Anthony, *Dream-Singers: The African American Way with Dreams*. John Wiley & Sons, Publishers, 2001

Smith, Theophus H. *Conjuring Culture: Biblical Formations of Black America*. Oxford University Press, 1994

Some, Malidoma Patrice. *The Healing Wisdom of Africa: Finding Life Purpose Through Nature, Ritual and Community*. New York: Jeremy P. Tarcher/Putnam, 1998

Sullivan, Martha Adams. "May the Circle Be Unbroken: The African-American Experience of Death, Dying and Spirituality." *A Cross-Cultural Look at Death, Dying, and Religion*. Eds. Joan K. Parry and Angela Shen Ryan. Chicago, IL: Nelson-Hall, 1995. 160-71.

Synan, Vinson. *The Holiness-Pentecostal Movement in the United States*. William B. Eerdmans Publishing Company, 1971

Teish, Luisah. *Jambalya: The Natural Woman's Book of Personal Charms and Practical Rituals*. San Francisco: Harper and Row, 1985
Thompson, Robert Farris. *Flash of the Spirit: African and Afro-American Art and Philosophy*. Random House, 1983

Thompson, Robert Farris. *Face of the Gods: Art and Altars of Africa and the African Americas*. Prestel, 1993

Thorton, John. *Africa and Africans in the Making of the Atlantic World, 1400-1800*. Cambridge University Press; 2 ed., 1998

Williams, Chancellor. *Destruction of Black Civilization: Great Issues of a Race from 4500 B.C to 2000 A.D.* Third World Press, 1987

Young, James T. *Rituals of Resistance: African Atlantic Religion in Kongo and the Lowcountry South in the Era of Slavery.* Louisiana State University Press, 2007

Index

A

Aakhu, 72, 75, 79, 82, 89, 129
Aapepu, 72, 76
Aha, (King Hru Aha), 62
Allan Kardec, 69
Alpha state of awareness, 52
Amun Ra, defined, 32
ancestral spirits. See Aakhu
Anubis. See Npu
archetype, 23, 73, 82, 100, 123, 136
atum, 36

C

Chango, 12, 137, 141, 142, 143, 150, 156, 160
Christian artifacts, 63
Christmas. See Rise of the King

D

Djahuti, 60, 74, 75, 83, 84, 85, 91, 129, 140, 145, 182, 185

E

Easter. See Return of Osar
Ellegua, 12, 154, 155, 156, 200

G

Good Friday. See Return of Osar, See Return of Osar

H

Haitian Revolution, 162
Hippolyte Léon Denizard Rivail. See Allan Kardec
Holiness, 209
Hru, 20, 21, 23, 24, 26, 59, 60, 61, 62, 63, 65, 74, 75, 85, 86, 90, 92, 129, 130, 140, 141, 142, 143, 181, 184, 185, 186, 187, 188, 199, 201, 203
Hruaakhuti, 59, 74, 75, 83, 85, 90, 93, 111, 158, 159, 160, 162, 163, 164, 181, 184, 185, 198
Hruur. See Hruaakahuti

K

Kamitic philosophy, 21, 31, 39
KhepeRa, defined, 35

M

Maat, 75, 76, 82, 83, 90, 158, 165, 166, 181, 201, 202

N

Nak. See Aapepu
Napoleon Hill, 123
Narmer, (King Narmer or Menes), 62
Nebertcher, 7, 30, 32, 39, 51, 52, 101
Nebhet, 25, 26, 58, 59, 74, 82, 85, 86, 91, 149, 150, 152, 153, 158, 180, 183, 184, 186, 187, 188
Netcharu, 72, 73, 82, 89
Npu, 59, 73, 74, 83, 84, 85, 86, 90, 153, 154, 155, 156, 157, 166, 180, 181, 182, 183, 189, 197

O

Obatala, 12, 134, 135, 141, 150, 200
Ogu. See Oggun
Ogun, 150, 151, 152, 156, 160
Orunmila, 138
Osar, 8, 21, 23, 29, 57, 58, 59, 60, 61, 62, 63, 73, 74, 75, 82, 84, 85, 86, 90, 111, 112, 116, 130, 134, 135, 136, 140, 150, 152, 153, 154, 163, 177, 180, 182, 183, 184, 185, 186, 187, 188, 201
Oset, 15, 16, 17, 58, 59, 60, 73, 82, 85, 86, 90, 136, 137, 138, 139, 153, 154, 158, 182, 183, 184, 185, 186, 187, 188, 189
Oshun, 13, 141, 150, 151, 152, 156

R

Ra Atum, defined, 35
Ra, defined, 32
Rau, 7, 36, 37, 52, 58, 70, 76, 84, 102, 103, 104, 105, 106, 107, 112, 113, 116, 118, 121

Return of Osar, 199
Rise of the King, 203
ritual, 31, 82, 88, 90, 97, 101, 124, 125, 126, 127, 131, 152, 153, 162, 171

S

Santeria, 208
Sebau,. *See* Aapepu
shu, 34, 36
Sokar, 75, 84, 91, 164, 167, 168, 170, 171, 180
soul loss, 24, 27

T

tefnut, 34, 36
Thoth. See Djahuti

trance, 13, 30, 52, 85, 95, 100, 126, 127, 128, 129, 130, 151, 197
Twilight. *See* Alpha state of awareness

U

Underground Railroad, 73

Y

Yemaya, 12, 137, 138, 151, 152
Yoruba, 7, 11, 13, 20, 134, 135, 137, 138, 141, 142, 150, 154

Made in the USA
Lexington, KY
17 May 2012